April 28, 1923–September 20, 2013

Carolyn Cassady graduated from Bennington College with a degree in Drama. She moved to Denver to pursue her Masters in Theater Arts; while there, she met and married Neal Cassady, who became known as the inspiration and muse for Jack Kerouac, Allen Ginsberg, and Ken Kesey. Carolyn was a prolific artist in her own right. Aside from enjoying painting, sculpting, drafting, block printing, embroidery, upholstering, and theater arts, she also published two memoirs, *Heart Beat* and *Off the Road*. She was fortunate enough to be able to pursue her passion for the theater as the Artistic Director for both the San Jose Light Opera Company and the Santa Clara University Drama Department. For many years, she designed stage sets, costumes, and hairstyles for the local dance school. When her three kids were grown and gone, Carolyn moved to England, where she lived her remaining thirty years.

"*Travel Tips for the Timid (Or, What Guide Books Never Tell)* by the illustrious Carolyn Cassady, is a charming narrative filled with heartfelt advice for adventurers and weary travelers alike! Evoking a bygone era of elegance and international travel that bursts with beauty and wonderment, you are invited to take a leisurely journey with a savvy mother and daughter team as they soak in the sites, culture, and deliciousness of each stop on an extended European Holiday. Incredible care and detail is given to each experience; you feel you can taste the wine and savor each meal as if you are hopping between train terminals with these lovely women. The book is filled with a wealth of delightful illustrations that help guide you through the journey. This travel memoir will inspire you to check your passport and seek an adventure of your own!"

—Heather Dalton, Producer and Director,
Neal Cassady: The Denver Years

"*Travel Tips* is great fun. I especially loved Carolyn's drawings in the book, where she captures the essence of life on her travels. As Carolyn and Jami found out, surprises—both good and bad—are what you remember best about a trip. Things that go smoothly are just not as much fun to remember years later. Also surprising to me, having known Carolyn since 1947, is that her poems in this book are so wonderful, and that they really showcase this facet of her many talents. This is a jewel of a book!"

—Al Hinkle, "Ed Dunkel" in Jack Kerouac's
On the Road

"*Travel Tips for the Timid* shows us that when it came time for the most famous woman of the Beat Generation to take the trip of a lifetime, she did so with characteristic grace and style. Her witty illustrations add to the fun of this delightful book."

—**Hilary Holladay, author of *Herbert Huncke: The Times Square Hustler Who Inspired the Beat Generation***

"Given the freewheeling group of Beat travelers who were her friends (and husband!) in her younger adult years, it's hard to believe that Carolyn Cassady was still an 'innocent abroad' when she set out for Europe for the first time in her mid-50s. This charming little book of travel tips is a record of Carolyn's ability to find the joy to be had in just about any situation, and her elegant, devil-may-care approach to seizing upon adventure. The drawings are delightful accompaniments to a chatty, friendly tale of finding one's way in a world where one must often depend on the kindness of strangers."

—**Elaine Katzenberger, Publisher, City Lights Books**

"Carolyn Cassady's remembrances of travels past is a rare slice of a rare life. Much more than a muse to husband Neal or to Jack Kerouac, Carolyn Cassady was a great artist whose body of work only grows in importance over time. *Travel Tips for the Timid* is a major new entry in the Beat canon I find both entertaining and illuminating."

—**Brenda Knight, author of *Women of the Beat Generation***

"Although I had corresponded with Carolyn Cassady for more than a decade, I never met her until the early 1980s when she visited New York City and stayed with my wife and I on the Lower East Side. On that and later visits, I experienced first-hand her love of art, conversation, and adventure in all forms. I knew of her abilities as an artist through her portraits of Allen Ginsberg, Jack Kerouac, and her husband Neal, but I wasn't familiar with her amazing talent as a quick-sketch artist which is now revealed in *Travel Tips*. Every page is a delight to read, savor, and admire. It is a charming and remarkable tell-all of what it was like to travel with this fascinating woman who always tells it like it is. Her desire to fully experience whatever she finds in her path is the key characteristic that comes through clearly in this delightful story of Americans abroad."

—Bill Morgan, author of *The Typewriter is Holy: The Complete, Uncensored History of the Beat Generation*

"Best known for her relationship to the legendary beat literati, Carolyn Cassady was an art student at the University of Denver when she went on the road with Neal Cassady, chronicling her life with Neal and Jack Kerouac in her memoirs *Heart Beat* and *Off the Road*. Kerouac reimagined her as 'Camille' in *On the Road* and famously joined the Cassady ménage in San Francisco when Neal and Carolyn were young parents.

"In the making of the movie of *On the Road*, director Walter Salles said his interview with Carolyn Cassady made him understand the heart of 'Dean,'

Kerouac's invented American hero. Yes, Camille plays the martyr, kicking Dean out in one breath and begging for his return in another, but the actress Kirsten Dunst (who portrayed 'Camille') said she did not think this a period detail; women go through the same disappointments today.

"Now, with this slim, precious volume from 1979, *Travel Tips for the Timid*, she does not reference her Beat past. Rather, Carolyn Cassady goes on the road with her daughter Jami, coming more into her own. In pictures and words, she returns to her creative roots; with whimsical drawings and observations of her European trip, she registers tourist fatigue and fascination with food and foreign customs. A time warp that is also quaint, charming and sincere in Cassady's own self-effacing voice."

—Regina Weinreich, author of *Kerouac's Spontaneous Poetics* and editor of Kerouac's *Book of Haikus*

TRAVEL TIPS

FOR THE *Timid*

Carolyn Cassady

Edited and introduced by Cathy Cassady Sylvia,
Jami Cassady Ratto, and John Cassady

Foreword by David Amram

Illustrations by Carolyn Cassady

OPEN BOOK PRESS
JACKSON COUNTY LIBRARY SERVICES
MEDFORD OREGON 97501

Some names and identifying details have been changed to protect the privacy of individuals.

www.theopenbookpress.com

Book design by Will Dane and Angela Sells
Original illustrations and images by Carolyn Cassady
Author photograph provided by Cathy Cassady

Library of Congress Cataloging-in-Publication Data

Names: Cassady, Carolyn—author; Cassady Sylvia, Cathy; John Cassady; Jami
    Cassady Ratto—editors.
Title: Travel Tips for the Timid: Or, What Guidebooks Never Tell / Carolyn
    Cassady.
Description: California: The Open Book Press, 2018.
Identifiers: LCCN 2018936195 (print)
ISBN-13: 978-0-9990414-6-8 (paperback) | 978-0-9990414-7-5 (e-book)
ISBN-10: 0-9990414-6-0 (paperback) | 0-9990414-7-9 (e-book)
Subjects: Travel Tips for the Timid—Beat Generation; History; Memoir; Poetry;
    Travel; Women's Studies.
Classification: TRAVEL/MEMOIR.

LC record available at https://lccn.loc.gov/2018936195

Printed in the United States of America

First Edition

THE OPEN BOOK PRESS is located at the Open Book, 671 Maltman Drive, Grass
    Valley, CA 95945

To our wonderful mother, Carolyn Cassady, who has been with us every step of the way as we resurrect her stories. Hearing Mom's voice through her writing has brought her back to life for us and reminded us what a disciplined, adventurous, and optimistic woman she was. This enchanting travel guide reveals the tenacity, wit and grace-under-pressure that exemplified our mother's approach to all the challenges she encountered during her long life. Heartfelt thanks to Mom for producing a voluminous collection of writing into which we're sure we will be gratefully delving for generations to come.

CONTENTS

ACKNOWLEDGMENTS

First of all, I have to thank the Universe for cooperating once again. Our Publishing Angel, Angela Sells, Ph.D. of The Open Book Press, was sent to us in a most serendipitous manner. In 2017, I opened the Sierra College adult education catalog and noticed a course being taught about women's roles in the Beat movement. That topic caught my attention as there is never a mention of "The Beats" in my conservative community. Wrong demographic.

Since our father was Neal Cassady, the inspiration for Dean Moriarty in Jack Kerouac's *On the Road*, I contacted the teacher, Angela, and asked if she'd be interested in having me speak to her class about what it was like growing up surrounded by the group of artistic souls known as "The Beats." She was, and I did.

Since Angela's degrees and passions lie with giving voice to women "whose stories—both fictional and factual—have been diminished or demeaned in history," my presentation covered the life and work of our accomplished mother, Carolyn Cassady, who has been one such historically "diminished" woman ("Meet the Author," *The Union*, November 10, 2017).

I did not discover until later that Angela and her partner, Will Dane, co-run a bookstore and The Open Book Press publishing house. We were astonished and feel blessed that this chance meeting resulted in our obtaining such a great gift from the Universe. We are eager to have our mother's talents recognized, and The

Open Book Press is eager to provide an avenue for that to happen.

It has been a delight working with Angela and Will. We cannot thank them enough for their skill, generosity, flexibility and thoroughness. They have been available at the drop of a hat and have patiently described the complicated process of publishing to us rookies. I have found that "A & W" don many hats during the extended publishing journey: as editors, promoters, agents, cheerleaders, instructors and hand-holders. We are forever grateful for their expertise and professionalism and look forward to working with them on future projects.

We are also most grateful to those generous souls who agreed to read a draft of *Travel Tips* and provide us with their kind comments:

A special THANK YOU is reserved for the great musician, composer, author, and creative genius, David Amram, who was extremely generous in providing the Foreword for *Travel Tips*. In between coming and going, going and coming, David managed to most graciously provide a wonderful testament to Mom's "zest for life, her devotion to her family, and her ability to overcome any struggles." David's enthusiasm and his own zest for life is reflected in the comments he offers. His contribution has enriched Mom's Tiny Tome, and we will be forever grateful.

Heather Dalton, Colorado PBS Producer and Director of the only Cassady-approved movie about our father, is a true friend. She worked tirelessly for years to bring the documentary, *Neal Cassady: The Denver*

Years to fruition. Over the years, Heather has part-nered with the us in promoting the Cassady legacy, and we truly appreciate her unfailing enthusiasm and will-ingness to join the team.

Al Hinkle ("Ed Dunkel"), the Last Man Standing, has been a lifelong friend of the Cassadys. He is nearly the only one left who was around when Dad and his cronies were causing such a ruckus in the 40s, 50s and 60s. We also appreciate the willing help of his daugh-ter, Dawn, who graciously added her comments.

Elaine Katzenberger, Executive Director of City Lights Books in San Francisco has been a part of the Cassadys' lives for decades. City Lights published our father's memoir, *The First Third*, and many of the groundbreaking works associated with the Beat move-ment. We were delighted that she was able to take time from her busy schedule to read and comment on Mom's travel guide.

Brenda Knight, the editor of the wonderful book, *Women of the Beat Generation,* among many others, has been most generous in her support and encourage-ment. We were fortunate to have met Brenda in 1996 when we joined Mom in the exciting events surround-ing the publication of *Women of the Beat Generation.* Brenda was way ahead of her time recognizing the ac-complishments and contributions made by the wom-en who were considered mere background noise to the men of the so-called "Beat Generation." We are happy to have Brenda in our corner.

Bill Morgan has been on the Beat trail for decades. If you Google Bill, you will see that he is the archivist and bibliographer for such prominent figures as Allen Ginsberg, Timothy Leary, and Lawrence Ferlinghetti. One of my favorite publications of his is *The Typewriter is Holy: The Complete, Uncensored History of the Beat Generation*. Bill went above and beyond to help us out. Just as we requested his input, he was leaving for a month-long trip to Italy, and despite being gone, he managed to read a rough draft and graciously add his thoughtful response to the book. We are most grateful.

Regina Weinreich is a Professor of Humanities and Science at The School of Visual Arts in New York. She is also a journalist, author, and filmmaker. Among her works: *Kerouac's Spontaneous Poetics*, Kerouac's *Book of Haikus*, and the documentary *Paul Bowles: The Complete Outsider*. She has written extensively about The Beats, and we feel truly fortunate that Regina agreed to read and offer her thoughts. We are most appreciative, and hope that we can meet Regina in the future and thank her in person.

Hilary Holladay, Ph.D., is a scholar of modern and contemporary American poetry and author of *Herbert Huncke: The Times Square Hustler Who Inspired Jack Kerouac and the Beat Generation*; "Huncke not only gave Jack Kerouac the word 'Beat,' but also introduced him to a truly beat world...and had an important impact on American literature" (Dennis McNally, author of *Desolate Angel: Jack Kerouac, the Beat Generation, and America*). We thank her for her contribution here.

I feel very lucky to have had the cooperation and enthusiastic support of my siblings, Jami Cassady Ratto and John Allen Cassady, throughout the process of transforming Mom's manuscript into book form. Since first setting eyes on her document years ago, I have wanted to see it in print. I love its humor, detailed descriptions, insight, and especially Mom's charming sketches. It seemed like a piece-of-cake assignment. All we needed to do was send her double-spaced typewritten draft to a publisher and it would be done, right?

Not so much. We discovered the whole thing needed to be re-typed, and of course my computer decided to die in the middle of the job. I could be sure of an empathetic ear as I vented to my siblings about that setback. The hours spent laboriously typing the 150 (small) pages from my mother's handwritten diary caused latent back and carpal tunnel issues to reappear. Siblings' shoulders were generously offered on which to lean. I could always count on cheerful encouragement from Jami and John when I was feeling overwhelmed, and a helpful suggestion when I was tapped out of ideas. It feels good to know you have my back. Thanks dear James and Li'l Bro.

I must also include a shout-out to our fabulous family and friends who followed our progress and offered continuing encouragement and pats on the back as we stumbled along. You'll never know how much your support has helped. Thank you all from the bottom of our hearts.

Lastly, but far from least, is the undying gratitude I have for my long-suffering, loving husband, George. His behind-the-scenes efforts were crucial to making this project a success. I am so impressed with his talents, I am going to embarrass him and describe the backstage magic he performed.

Without complaint, he took on the duty of scanning Mom's 162-page scrapbook into the computer. Since the pages are 12" x 12," he had to scan four sections per page to equal one digital page. He re-paginated the digital version of the scrapbook, which caused untold grief when I was searching for certain pages as I typed the manuscript. George therefore created a spreadsheet reference guide for me which included the original page number, the new digitized page number, and the page numbers corresponding to each country Mom and Jami visited. This document was a life-saver as I checked, re-checked and triple-checked the scrapbook reference pages in the manuscript.

It took hours of matching, patching and Paint Shop Pro-ing for George to make each colorful scrapbook page as beautiful online as it looks in-person, so to speak. He also scanned the entire handwritten travel diary into the computer, and the illustrated typewritten original manuscript. The entire document is now digitized. Thanks to George, we are back in the 21st century! His was a comforting presence throughout the project. George has my gratitude in perpetuity for his forbearance, devotion, ongoing encouragement, creative problem-solving, and most of all, for his reliable talent for making me laugh. This book would not have seen the light of day without our dear Geo.

EDITORS' BIOGRAPHIES

Cathy Cassady Sylvia

Cathy Cassady was born in San Francisco, California. Her childhood was spent in the South Bay Area in Monte Sereno. After high school, Cathy spent twenty years working as a medical assistant and transcriber before returning to college. Having spent most of her working years sitting down, she realized it was not a healthy way for folks to spend their days. She thus earned a B.S. in Exercise Physiology, and an M.S. in Worksite Wellness Management. She spent the rest of her career as a health educator, helping employees stay healthy and fit.

She is currently retired, living with her husband, George, and their loveable Labradoodle, Tula, near their three kids and six grandchildren in Northern California.

Jami Cassady Ratto

Jami, Carolyn and Neal's middle child, has been married to Randy Ratto for 43 years. They have one child, Becky, and three beautiful grandchildren. In 2015, Jami retired from 48 years in the dental field. She now has more time to pursue her passions which not only include her family, but also helping the world to know and care about the Cassady Legacy. Jami lives in Santa Cruz, California.

John Allen Cassady

Born on September 9, 1951 in San Francisco, California, John Allen Cassady is the third of Carolyn and Neal Cassady's three children.

After attending Saratoga High School and West Valley College, John worked in a variety of trades, including metal worker, welder, wood worker, luthier, musical instrument builder, and computer programmer. He worked for 16 years at Caere Corporation, which made Optical Character Recognition and bar code scanners. Now retired, John is currently writing a book about growing up with Neal and his family and friends, with a working title of *Visions of Neal: A Boy's Life With His Father.*

John currently lives in Willow Glen, California with his son Jamie, wife Michelle, and his grandchildren Cody and Carly.

INTRODUCTION

Imagine a dream you've had for over fifty years. Close your eyes and imagine that dream coming true. Now feel the joy. The tiny tome you hold in your hands is the expression of such Joy. When she was 56 years old, our mother, Carolyn Cassady, was finally able to take the trip of her dreams and share it with her middle child, Jami. They wandered through Europe for two months soaking in all the history and culture they could. Carolyn was so extremely delighted to have the opportunity to take this trip, that she documented their experiences in every way imaginable. Her excitement and awe are contagious, as you will discover.

The journey was taken in 1979. Carolyn had extra funds at that time since she'd been hired as a consultant on the movie *Heart Beat*, which was based on an excerpt from her memoir. (The completed work, *Off The Road: Twenty Years with Neal Cassady, Jack Kerouac and Allen Ginsberg*, was published in 1990.) After filming wrapped, Carolyn and Jami took off for their once-in-a-lifetime trip to (hopeful) favorite places in Europe. Little did they know that four years later, Carolyn at age 60, "ran away from home," as she put it, and lived the next thirty years in England until her death on September 20, 2013. It's interesting to read her impressions of the countryside surrounding the coastal towns of Hastings and Rye, because her first home in England was in Winchelsea, which is between those two towns.

Carolyn Elizabeth Robinson was born on April 28, 1923 in Lansing, Michigan. She was the youngest of five children born to biochemist Dr. Charles S. Robinson and Florence Sherwood, a former high school English teacher. The arts, literature, and education were highly regarded, and every one of the Robinson children earned graduate degrees. The family moved to Tennessee when Carolyn was eight years old, due to her father's career move to Vanderbilt University as head of the Biochemistry Department. Since her parents were educators and they had summers off, she was able to spend every summer at Glen Lake in Michigan, even after their move to Nashville.

Carolyn earned a scholarship to Bennington College in Vermont after graduating from Ward Belmont Preparatory School for Girls in Nashville. At Bennington, which at the time was a private women's college, she began studying art, but switched to drama, receiving her BA in Stanislavsky Drama in 1944.

After college, she became an Occupational Therapist for the Army until World War II ended. In 1946, she went to Denver to study for her MA degree in Fine Arts and Theater Arts. While in Denver, she met Neal Cassady—whom she later married—and became involved in the group subsequently known as the Beats, which included Jack Kerouac, Allen Ginsberg, and Joyce Johnson, among other notable writers and artists.

Throughout her life, Carolyn's creativity was expressed in seemingly limitless ways. She enjoyed painting, sculpting, gardening (one summer designing a twelve-zone garden based on astrology charts), drafting, block printing, embroidery (creating her own designs), sewing, upholstering, and all theater arts; she designed award-winning stage sets, costumes, makeup, and hairstyles. As is often the case, we children took her talents for granted. Mom was always busy.

We knew she created colorful astrology charts for friends and family. There was the ubiquitous smell of oil paints in the house with someone always sitting for a portrait in our living room. She experimented with art projects using various media. We read aloud to her as she sewed costumes she'd designed for theatrical productions as well as our dance company performances. In her later years, we were not surprised to see gorgeous paintings on her cabinets and walls in her London flat and in the house for which she had designed the floor-plan and garden.

All this was old hat. We knew she had two memoirs published which chronicled the twenty years she was involved with the Beats: *Heart Beat* and *Off the Road*. (The movie version of *Heart Beat* starred Sissy Spacek as Carolyn and Nick Nolte as Neal Cassady.) She kept up a voluminous correspondence and continued to write long-hand letters and emails on her computer at home to family, friends, and hundreds of fans from all over the world, until the end. She never failed to answer a letter and was always gracious to those seeking advice and counsel. She accomplished all this while holding down full-time jobs, caring for three children and a home, and dodging the authorities as Dad and his pals wreaked various forms of havoc. Her goal, and we children can attest to its relative success, was to bring us up in as "normal" an environment as she could. Needless to say, it was a challenge.

After she passed away, Jami, John, and I were astounded to discover the fantastic treasures our mother had accumulated during her productive 90 years. Aside from the sketches and drawings and art work, we uncovered evidence of her prolific writing: volumes of correspondence, journals, poignant poetry reflecting her loneliness while living in England, at least one screenplay, a 600-page typed autobiography, advice columns and news articles from her journalistic ventures, a novel or two, and this delightful travel memoir. We had no idea she had been industriously toiling away at these other endeavors "behind our backs," so to speak.

If we had any doubt before, finding the extensive documentation of her European trip convinced us that Carolyn was detail-oriented and disciplined, as well as creative. The thrill of traveling to the places she'd studied and heard about since childhood was so great, she did not want one second to go undocumented if she could help it. She set down her impressions in multiple ways (full versions available online at tinyurl.com/cassadytips. Password: TopWithens).

1) An illustrated travelogue: Carolyn returned home from her journey and gleefully created the original *Travel Tips for the Timid*. She describes experiences and challenges she and Jami encountered throughout the trip in various locales with the goal of easing the way for future travelers. Each chapter describes issues regarding transportation, accommodations, meals, etc.

in every country they visited. These challenges are revealed in a light-hearted way accompanied by charming illustrations.

2) Travel Diary (italicized text): from a handwritten travel diary kept throughout the trip. Carolyn wrote these notes in a 4" x 6" alphabetized address book she kept with her. (E = England, I = Italy, etc.) She jotted down her impressions either while bouncing along on public transportation, at the end of the day in their hotel room, or whenever she found a spare moment. She documented overheard conversations, stories, details of the décor, food, and people of each region. Some of these diary entries appear as thoughts in prose; others as notes which are interwoven throughout the main manuscript and are italicized. Though at times repetitive, the diary entries add color and flavor to the trip, revealing Carolyn's passions, attitudes and opinions. The diary appears in full without interruption in Appendix A, and a few samples of the original handwritten pages in Appendix C.

3) Scrapbook: as if the illustrated document and the travel diary do not provide enough detail, a link is provided to the 162 page, 12" x 12" scrapbook generated from the trip. It is organized chronologically from the first day of their tour to the last day heading back home. Carolyn was a collector and that talent is displayed admirably here. She kept every scrap of napkin, ticket, brochure, photo, postcard and magazine article she came across on their journey. All these are included in the scrapbook, including the photos they took. The cameras in 1979 still used film, which had to be developed

upon their return, and as one can see, the photos do not do justice to the beauty they encountered. In case these did not adequately describe an event or situation, Carolyn added handwritten notes and sketches to illustrate the scene or point she was trying to make. A list of scrapbook images that coincide with specific passages in the text is provided at the end of each chapter. Please see tinyurl.com/cassadytips for full access to every scrapbook page. Enter password: TopWithens.

4) Maps: a separate page of maps is included in the scrapbook and here in Appendix B.

It is obvious Carolyn wants us along for the ride. She is eager to share her delight and astonishment at the fun she and Jami are experiencing. She had a way of seeing the humor in situations that others might not appreciate. As with many complicated endeavors, a long trip such as this is fraught with perils. Mom saw the absurdity of everyday life and would often lighten otherwise grim circumstances by pointing this out. (I feel her talent in this area was honed by the strong British-related upbringing she had. We children share this love of all things British, especially the dry humor. We were raised to believe that when you die and go to Heaven...it's Britain.) As she reviewed the trip, she realized they had many experiences that required a "we'll laugh about this later" attitude. And they did. I am happy she decided to put those situations in written form, so we can now share in the chuckles.

Her artist's eye is revealed at every turn. Her words paint pictures of the beauty surrounding them. She describes their meals, the colors and décor of each room, the details of clothing, and attitudes of the people they encountered. Her passions are apparent: architecture, art, health, nutrition, nature, history, spirituality, human nature, museums, galleries, performing arts, clothing, and hairstyles. She gets to wallow in them all, and we are joyfully carried along. (We know she would be "chuffed" if readers succumbed to their own creative urges and colored the black and white sketches included in the book.)

Being written in pre-technology 1979 before the advent of smart phones, the internet or Google Maps, this is rather like an historical document. A similar journey taken today would most likely not include some of the challenges they encountered. For example: the luggage would have been far less of a problem, and not as heavy. Carolyn states, "we did wonder why these few cases could be so heavy. The tape recorder was a small one, as were the calculator and clock radio." They were hauling "maps, guidebooks, notebooks, phrasebooks, menu masters, doctor directories, hotel and hostel guides..." all of which would today be included in a smart phone, tablet, or even a hi-tech watch.

Jami and Carolyn had to look up information in paper form—books, maps, brochures, programs, etc. They were at the mercy of the weather and were sometimes unprepared since they could not use a weather app to research future forecasts. Occasionally they had to find a phone booth to contact people, for which they sometimes had to wait in line. They were often lost and had to deal with last-minute changes in schedules or unexpected office closures which today we avoid by looking up information online. The currency was different from today's as well: there was no such thing as the EU with its Euro, so every time they crossed a border they had to exchange currency, which did not always go smoothly. They had to rely on accommodations being available at the last minute since they could not look up hotels on the 'net or call on their cell phones to get immediate answers. They did a lot of wandering from hotel to hotel in search of adequate rooms. The good news: they didn't gain a pound despite eating multi-course meals at nearly every stop. There are advantages to wandering.

Of course, the lack of technology added to the fun and excitement of this adventure. As Carolyn recounts in one section, whenever she and Jami began complaining about some aggravating circumstance or person, they'd say, "pinch, pinch" as a reminder to wake up and appreciate where they were and what a marvelous opportunity this trip was. It is heartwarming to share their journey. Editing these documents was a thrill for those of us who were not able to join them. We felt, as I hope you will, that we were negotiating those cobblestone streets and craning our necks in awe at the marvelous architecture and scenery just as they were.

Bon Voyage!

Cathy Cassady Sylvia

Our mother, Carolyn Elizabeth Robinson Cassady, was first and foremost, above all else, an artist, in every realm that the title implies. She was a painter, illustrator, portrait artist, set designer, costume designer, makeup artist, seamstress, writer, poet, author, driver, story teller, loving wife and mother, and so much more. She sold her portraits of the neighborhood kids, done in charcoal or pastels, to their parents for $50 each, which helped put me and my two older sister through school. ($50 was big cake in the '50s!) Her masterpiece was a full-sized color portrait, done in oil, of my high school sweetheart, Ellen. Her parents gave mom $300 for that one—a steal, considering the hours spent at the easel, and for Ellen's sitting for it, with myself as a distraction.

There can still be found, in the borders of pages in her favorite books, her sketches of the characters and costumes that she imagined were in the stories, which included the complete set of Oz books. Simply remarkable.

She meant the World to me, her only son, and although she passed in 2013, aged 90, in her beloved England, her spirit lives on, for now and forever, in the hearts, souls, minds and prayers of us all. She is truly missed.

I'll eventually join you, mum, (albeit hopefully not too soon), in the great hereafter, so hold on— I'm coming—and we'll be together again.

**Love always,
John Allen Cassady**

FOREWORD

For those of us fortunate enough to have known Carolyn Cassady, we wish people of today's generation could have had the pleasure of spending time with this remarkably feisty, independent, and talented woman.

Now, thanks to the publication of *Travel Tips for the Timid,* her classic memoir *Off the Road* is joined by a new series of adventure stories, as she shows her daughter (and all of us readers) the joys of traveling uncharted paths and gracefully overcoming all the bumps in the road.

Reading *Travel Tips* makes it is possible to get to know Carolyn through her own words as she paints a picture for all of us of her zest for life, her devotion to her family and her ability to overcome any struggles we face in life by improvising as a way to resolve all setbacks.

Travel Tips enables you to go on the road with Carolyn and understand why so many people loved being with her.

This delightful series of vignettes also shows that rather than ever taking the easy path, she spent her life being honest. She never succumbed to role playing or self-aggrandizement and refused to allow herself to ever wallow in Whineology or Blameology when she was overlooked as Neal Cassady and Jack Kerouac became Pop caricatures of themselves.

Throughout her long life, she always remained true

to herself and avoided the quagmire of literary politics.

She was a life-long advocate of keeping it real, and she made sure that whenever you were with her, you tried to do the same.

Her stories in this book make you understand her purity of spirit and her ability to laugh in the face of setbacks and always find a way to deal with adversity.

Her straightforward way of living life explains why she refused to become a stereotype in order to profit either herself or her family (by becoming an official representative of a non-existent movement). Instead, she was an advocate for celebrating the yea-saying spirit of Jack Kerouac, the endless energy of her husband Neal, and the celebration of creativity in all people. Over the years, she honored the friendships she made with people from all walks of life!

When her precious children were grown, she moved to England. In addition to returning to oil painting, she spent endless hours answering anonymous letters, e-mails, and phone calls from people around the world.

I always enjoyed seeing her every time I was in England, as well as whenever she came back to the USA to participate in events that honored our Era. I say "Era," because like Jack, Neal, Lawrence Ferlinghetti, Gregory Corso, myself and countless others, she despised the term "Beat Generation," seeing it as a catchall way to marginalize and dismiss many unique people by lumping them all together in a franchised slop pit of mediocrity.

Whenever the events we participated in were over, we would stay up until dawn, sharing stories about the priceless times of our Era, usually joined by young people who were inspired by the freedom and joy of life that they sensed we experienced.

One such moment has always stayed with me throughout the years: we were both elders-in-residence for a celebration of the Kerouac Writers' Residence in Florida; the little bungalow in College Park, where Jack and his mother shared a tiny room, was being turned into a writers' residence. This humble little home was where Jack returned after the extraordinary success of *On the Road* to write *The Dharma Bums*.

Journalist-newscaster-author Bob Kealing, one of the founders of the Writers' Residence, arranged an all-night televised interview wherein Carolyn and I spoke and were spoken to for hours by a large group of anyone who cared to show up. We heard a series of amazing untold stories by Ronnie Low, who befriended Jack in his last years and was with him the night he died. He and Carolyn swapped priceless tales of their escapades for hours, and suddenly, a Florida version of Homer's rosy-fingered dawn began to light up the sky.

"Carolyn," I said, trying to be diplomatic and respectful. "It's getting kind of late. Don't you think... maybe....you should get some rest and call it a day, now that the new one has arrived?"

"Definitely NO," she said, lighting another cigarette and pouring herself another tumbler of white wine. "I'm afraid I might miss something."

Now Carolyn has left us, and the video tape and the man who shot it have disappeared, but *Travel Tips for the Timid* has arrived!

When people have continued to ask me over the years what Jack Kerouac was really like, I always say, "Read his books. That's *exactly* what he was like."

For all of you who would like to know what Carolyn was like, I suggest that you read *her* books!

And I suspect that those of you who have kids (and even grandkids) will find that they, too, will enjoy *Travel Tips for the Timid* as much as you do.

Thanks to the Cassady family, The Open Book Press, and its founders Will Dane and Angela Sells; we can now all spend some time with Carolyn every time we read and re-read this delightful new book.

David Amram

Composer, conductor, writer, and author of *Offbeat: Collaborating with Kerouac*

Even as I look back now, after about 40 years, it still amazes me that I was able to accompany my mother to Europe! She had received a sum of money from a Hollywood movie company to make a movie from her small portion of a larger book in process. The movie was called Heart Beat and starred Nick Nolte as her husband, Neal Cassady, Sissy Spacek as herself, Carolyn Cassady, and John Heard as their friend, Jack Kerouac. Mom's larger work was published in 1990 and is called Off The Road, Twenty Years with Cassady, Kerouac and Ginsberg.

I was 29 at the time we set off, 1979, married since 1975 to my husband, Randy. I had been in the field of dentistry for about ten years but was able to get time off to join mom on her adventure.

And what an adventure it was!

We took a tour for the first leg of the journey, as neither of us had been "across the pond" before. The tour was very helpful and we learned a lot.

Then we were on our own for the rest of the trip, and did really well!

She made this wonderful book after we came home and after all these years it still brings back such amazing memories… I still laugh at the funny cartoons.

Yes, it certainly was one of the most special times in my life.

I am so glad that my sister has tackled this project and you can enjoy mom's travel tips book.

I think our trip actually helped mom decide to move to England when she was 60 years old. She lived there in her dream home until she passed in 2013 at the age of 90.

Jami Cassady Ratto

TRAVEL TIPS

FOR THE *Timid*

OR, WHAT GUIDEBOOKS NEVER TELL

PREFACE

"GO ABROAD": throughout my life, into my fifties, a Siren's Call. Continental Europe and the British Isles had been the sources of all the art, literature and history that ever inspired me, but my travels had remained limited to the printed page. Not until I was fifty-six could I actually visit those sources, and my patience was rewarded with the joyful accompaniment of my twenty-nine-year old daughter Jami.

If you hesitate to take the plunge "abroad," the notes that follow are for you. The first lesson we learned, when we started traveling, was that travel books and brochures, intent on getting you there or signing you up, tend to omit many aspects of travel that we would have preferred to know about in advance. "Why didn't anyone tell us?" became a chant as surprise followed surprise.

The courageous, the self-reliant might find the matters in question too insignificant to mention, and the seasoned traveler might have forgotten the initial shocks of discoveries, but to the faint of heart, as we once were, I offer a few of our experiences in the pages that follow, to help smooth the way. For "go abroad" everyone should, and the sooner the better.

We visited Portugal, Spain, Italy, France, England and Scotland, with brief glimpses of Morocco and Switzerland. We're wary now and braced for surprises elsewhere, should we get the chance to go again.

Throughout the two months prior to take-off, we prepared the best we could. We bought travel books, guidebooks, maps, and magazines, and haunted the library and our traveling friends. We then decided to buy a 60-day airline excursion ticket, and began—playing it safe—with a guided three-week tour of Portugal and Spain. We planned to strike out on our own over the remaining five weeks.

We knew we must "travel light"—everyone said so—but how could we know what we'd need in six different countries from late March through May? We were all packed, our bags full of clothes suitable for California in April and May, when the Fates sent in two weeks of cold rain that inspired us to check foreign weather charts again. We repacked: thermal underwear (an absolute must; we wore it every night and on some days), sweaters and more sweaters, heavy slacks, socks, gloves, rainwear and of course, the unanimously recommended "onepairofsturdywalkingshoes." We discarded anything that needed ironing and any electrical gadgets that required converters. We sorted and re-sorted until we were down to one medium-sized, lightweight suitcase apiece, one shoulder bag with multiple compartments each, and one (required) flight bag each, one of which we stowed in a suitcase.

Several sources encouraged us to pack "basic" blacks and greys, with scarves and jewelry to jazz them up. Later on, after carrying these frills around for weeks, we realized that we lacked the knack some women have with scarves. (I had also given Jami a booster permanent hair style at the last minute before

traveling—and left it on too long. "Good thing the 'Afro' is in," she sighed.)

While patting ourselves on the back for our baggage efficiency, we did wonder why these few cases could be so heavy. The tape recorder was a small one, as were the calculator and clock radio. One had to pack shampoo, rinse, toothpaste and brush, soap, curlers, hand/face cream, nail stuff, deodorants, combs and hairbrushes, Band-Aids, aspirin, cough drops, inhalers, vitamin pills, cologne, laundry detergent plus clothespins, line, and inflatable hangers: light weight, all of it. None of these things were heavy—not as heavy as the books turned out to be. Maps, guidebooks, notebooks, phrasebooks, menu masters, doctor directories, hotel and hostel guides... The clothes were the least of our burden.

Throughout the trip, because Jami wore a cape, she carried the hand luggage, and I the shoulder-strapped bags—giving us each an interesting new posture.

And a new problem arose when traversing train doorways and bus aisles.

As soon as we left the guided tour for our five weeks of independence, we packed one suitcase full of the jewelry, scarves, inflatable hangers and clothes lines, etc., as well as the souvenir booklets we'd collected at every site, and shipped the whole lot home. This left us with only four pair of slacks, six pullovers, a black cardigan and a blue one, two or three sleeveless shells for "layering," two pairs of boots, and two of walking shoes. We both wear the same sizes, so we would mix and match these for the rest of the trip.

Since we would no longer be seeing the same people every day, only we would know.

From the plane

Circumscribed cumulus clouds
against the shadow of our plane encircled
by a rainbow orb. Beneath, the neat new green
    fields,
red earth dotted with clusters of red-roofed
    white houses,
splashes of sandstone cliffs, a birthmark forest
and the broad yellow Tagus River,
washing hanging from every window on long
    lines.

Carolyn's diaries throughout are in *italics*.

See Page 1 of the Scrapbook (and all other scrapbook images) online at **tinyurl.com/cassadytips**

Click on the Scrapbook link
and enter password **TopWithens**

ONE

Getting There

(You Can't Get There From Here)

A T THE BEGINNING: off we went, armed with secure
confidence in our guidebooks' and brochures' re-
assurances...but even before we'd de-planed at Kennedy Airport in New York, we uttered our first "but we
were told that..."

In flight, it became clear that we would arrive in
New York late. Our travel agent had said that in such
an event the pilot would call ahead to our connecting
airline—the tour's flight from Kennedy—and inform
them we were on our way. When we first asked the
flight attendant to communicate with the pilot, she said
she couldn't go into the cabin at that time. The second
time, as we approached New York, she said she had to
sit down and fasten her seat belt for landing. So, on arrival, we had twenty minutes to make our connecting
flight on the Portuguese airline TAP, having been told

to do so at least an hour beforehand.

On our way off the plane, we asked the flight attendant what we should do. "Ask the man in the suit inside," was her response.

There's only one man in a suit? we wondered, and asked the first likely one we saw. He pointed to the Information Desk. We had no idea where TAP was, and it was obvious we'd get no help from TWA; their Information Desk was surrounded by travelers and staffed with only one attendant...with our time running out.

We remembered that our tour instructions included a verification number, and we leapt into a phone booth and dialed.

"Bom dia, Senhora," came the melodic voice.

We told her of our plight.

"Don't worry; your plane has not yet arrived from Lisbon. We are only three buildings away from where you are, in the British Airways terminal."

No one had told us about the yellow jitneys that carry passengers to-and-fro around the airport. We grabbed our luggage and walked out into a dark, raging Nor'easter, our umbrella and rain bonnets (of course) neatly packed away. In our high-heeled boots ("We'll only be sitting on a plane") we clambered over torn-up pavement, dodged puddles and blinking barricades, and leaned into the slashing gale for what seemed like miles, arriving at the TAP desk like proverbial drowned rats, indeed, and shivering with cold. Our careful plans to appear at our best to our fellow tourists were literally down the drain.

TAP
Forget your troubles...
get TAP-happy!

We had not understood that the foremost reason travelers sign up for tours is to shop. On our tour, Jami and I turned out to be the only virgin travelers (pardon the expression), and our motives were purely educational and soul-enriching. Since our baggage would be handled for us only the first three of eight weeks, space was at a premium. Others on the tour, whose travels were limited to those three weeks, could bring the maximum allowed, with clothing suitable for any occasion in a limited area, and acquire any other goodies they liked. Jami and I resisted the wares the tour guides thrust upon us...or most of them, anyway; and we had no flowing gowns to wear to dinner. At first, we wondered why we were scheduled to stay two or three days in busy cities and only a few hours in places with more charm or history. Then we caught on: shopping opportunities [next page].

In Morocco (a 30-hour side trip from Spain), for instance, our local guide urged on the driver in order to get to a bazaar in Tangier and ensure his cut from what the shoppers would buy. Once we got there, haggling was the order.

Any tour must nurture regrets that there is so little time, but on the whole (aside from the above), we were pleased with our plan; it seemed as leisurely and balanced as possible, as, during the tour, we took note of places to return to during our independent weeks, in lieu of tearing our hair out. And the benefit of the quick stops was that we covered a lot of ground, and our guides tended to be generous with their knowledge.

Stray Thoughts

Aljezur was a pretty village, old wall, most pop-ular tour, north of the ocean, village pines eucalyp-tus. Zambujeira, all trip scenery terrific. Casa Branca view toward the sea; land confiscated by communists. (Mostly state-owned, perhaps.) Vasco de Gama was born at the Sines resort. Santiago de Cacém for lunch, roof of four levels. Story of a stork: a little boy wanted a little brother. Why didn't you tell the bird you want-ed one? A woman and St. Peter, no, wrong, used to be an angel word, no, a chicken. A W.C. and an English lady in Switzerland are looking for a room. Khrush-chev and Kennedy telephone a bell, it cost $101.

We realized early in the tour that in school we'd been exposed to little history of Spain and none of Por-tugal. And Jami did not understand the geography of the whole hemisphere. Thankfully, our guides could fire up one's interest with their enthusiasm, and we were delighted we'd chosen these neglected countries to tour with guides who made the education an exciting adventure.

In Iberia, there is one thing you can count on: your train or bus will invariably arrive at your destination either at the onset of siesta or after closing hours. The custom of buttoning up every place for two or three hours after noon is becoming less universal, but this only ensures that you'll forget about it the next time, and still won't be able to get that essential aspirin, money, directions, or meal.

Advertisements for "The American Express Experience" had lulled us into believing the AE office was every American's mother away from home. Even when we could sleuth out the location of the office (frequently hiding behind another name), we often found it closed, or open but staffed with locals not necessarily understanding our side. For instance, after leaving the tour in Lisbon we had planned to go to the northwestern corner of Spain and thence along the coast to San Sebastian, but in Lisbon, neither the AE office nor the local Tourismo office would share any knowledge of Spain.

It was the end of the tour. We drove over what must have been gorgeous shoreline, but the windows were so wet that the breakers looked like rick-rack. The rain drowned a small car; its angry little horn complained for minutes. Jami and I tried to find American Express and a Tourism Office. We skipped our venture downtown and got all mixed up, having been given the wrong directions. Instead, we had port at a café before starting back.

We just happened to look up to find the Tourism Office we'd been looking for. Bank of America changed our money; all of the other banks were closed. The [clerk] had us into a new hotel and half way out of Portugal in minutes. The directions Hella gave us were slipping. We tried to check with her Friday afternoon, but the lines were busy and there was too much rain, so we had to stay over on Monday. Still, all so much simpler than we feared—great relief.

During the gala dinner, we got group pictures and exchanged addresses (Jami began passing them around). Everyone was so nice and sad under a big, full moon. We were on the top floor, which didn't help our colds. We had cream of asparagus soup, Coquille St. Jacques, a real steak, some frozen dessert, and two kinds of wine. Freedom now! [She and Jami at this point depart from their tour group and venture off as a twosome.]

On Saturday morning, we called the Diplomático and they said our rooms would be ready when we were. We had a huge breakfast in the room, packed, and were out of the Altis by 10:30. We've been tipping too much in fear, even though it says service included. Ah well. The Diplomático hotel was nice, if not elegant. It was homier with decorative tile in the bedroom, a massage device on the bed, a dressing room bigger than Altis, a balcony, a royal blue carpet, and flowered wallpaper with white rock roses on a mustard ground. There were red and blue dots on the water faucets, room radios, and elevators. The staff was relaxed and friendly. There was also a nice little gift shop, bar, and restaurant with a coffee shop—fast service.

Miserable with the cold, so I couldn't get out to look at the Portuguese sky. It is all one world, we are all God's children; OK, so the same sky may be over California, but those fluffy white clouds are Portuguese, and Lisbon's alone. That crooked moon last night the same moon, yes, but with a Portuguese slant. Don't argue. Sudden shafts of golden sun, though it showered continually. There must be a land of rainbows somewhere beyond the square buildings that face us.

Oh yes, the lamp posts! Last night in the nine-story restaurant, we looked down on them and on our little street; galleons perched atop. Little crows on the side streets, but Castilho Street had the galleons.

Remember:
Men setting tile on Avenida da Liberdade
scratching their heads
Piles of rubble
Looking down from my balcony, I see the
sidewalks
(White, grey, black)

Old men sit amidst the traffic,
hacking away at the stone to get them into shape
Every street made by hand
No camera

The American Express was a total bust. The clerk
said simply that there were no buses traveling north
to Madrid. We were booked at a Pousada near Aveiro
with no idea how to get there. Take a train to Aveiro,
then what? No one would talk about Spain. [Portu-
guese Pousadas and Spanish Paradors are govern-
ment-owned accommodations in renovated historic
buildings such as convents, monasteries, castles, and
fortresses.]

Views of Oporto from the four-cornered win-
dows were like "find the face" pictures—every time
we looked, we saw something different: aqueducts,
churches, vacant lots above busy streets, incredible
slums with new additions, dogs, cats, goats. The ra-
dio reception was poor; we tuned to classical, jazz, or
country and got either only bass or melody. Drinks
were double what they were only two months ago: $4
each for gin!

It is difficult to plan cross-country travel when half
the nation's public transportation isn't running, and
you can make no allowances for the delays caused by
layovers. Naturally, if you're brave, then driving your-
self is the answer, and I can hear the clamor, "Rent a
car, rent a car you dummies." You're not serious. Us?
We panic enough in any wheeled conveyance; we're not
about to try and compete in a strange car on strange
roads with no speed limits. On foot you're not safe,

either. In Barcelona, we ran a gauntlet of automobile traffic twice a day, for three days, across the Plaza de San Jaime.

Here and in other cities we'd be walking along a two-foot-wide sidewalk, jostling other pedestrians against the wall or stepping off the curb, when a car would suddenly appear coming straight at us on the sidewalk. If there's no parking spot on the street, drivers tend to adjust; but it's a bit off-putting, I must say. On the other hand, in London streets we were grateful for the consideration shown in big white hints on the pavement to let you know from whence you're likely to be mowed down.

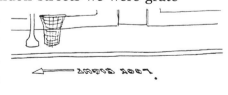

We'd read about Portugal's taxi drivers, but we were forced to entrust our lives to them a number of times, anyway. Still, we felt a lot happier to be inside their cars rather than competing with them in another. We had to hire one for a twenty-mile drive to a Pousada, and another the next day to a ten-mile train connection. Close

to the Pousada, we were amused by a sign warning "pavimento undulato" quite unnecessarily. We gained practice testing theories on how to overcome fear.

In Oporto, when we needed a taxi to get us and our luggage from the train station to our hotel, we couldn't convince one to take us, even though it was early afternoon, and the hotel was within walking distance of the station. We lacked a map of the town, and one taxi driver pantomimed that it was too close to be worth his while. The shortest distance between the two points turned out to be straight up a hill—but we couldn't understand his directions at the time. We stood confused on the street corner. Then we noticed a strawberry vendor, and Jami wrote the name of the hotel on a piece of paper and handed it to her. This rosy lady smiled and nodded and dropped a few coins into Jami's outstretched hand. Afterward, we surmised she couldn't read and had responded to the familiar gesture as usual. Then from different directions three men came running, each trying to outdo the other in helpfulness.

The winner led us within sight of the hotel. We decided it would be insulting to offer him money; we'd met with this level of generosity everywhere in Portugal.

We had not planned to spend a night in Oporto, but the train out ran only once a day at 4:43 p.m., and that day's had just left, while we waited out the siesta hours. We regretted sacrificing sight-seeing in this historical city, but we were unfamiliar with it and decided to use the 24 hours to rest our colds and to wash heavier clothing that might now have time to dry.

The following afternoon we were on our way again...

...with plenty of time to spare.

The train cleaning crew asked us (in sign language) to wait on the platform, then, when they'd finished, called us back in and sat with us, pointing out how alike we looked.

We showed them postcard pictures of San Francisco.

Then, at 4:35 p.m....

We weren't about to walk up the numerous steps to the hotel; we *had* to find a taxi this time. We did, and we caught our train, too. Luckily, it made another stop across town.

One of several experiences with instant translation:

We enjoyed the history and novelty of most of the unfamiliar customs and foreign traditions we encountered on our trip. But we found train compartments— which in films had looked so romantic—to be anything but. Strangers sit face-to-face staring at each other, bumping knees or trodding on feet if escape becomes imperative. If you're out to make friends, well and good. We found many, but privacy is something we prize as well, and the setting is confining and uncomfortable. Some of the older passenger cars in more remote areas offered only two rows of woven seats and wood flooring—no compartments at all. On these, the local color was more evident, and we learned to adopt the local custom of bringing along a lunch.

In Oporto, we bought a cross-country ticket to San Sebastian, on the northern coast of Spain near the French border. We hoped to recoup at least one of our losses by staying in the Parador there (one more night in Spain). On the train, we soon learned the disadvantages of riding backwards in a compartment. Our new Portuguese student friend spoke English well, but for some reason didn't tell us our station was coming up,

and afterward insisted we really didn't want to get off anyway. The trainmen hadn't announced the stations either.

We were distressed to have missed the stop, and apprehensive about then entering France without a ticket and our francs all safely packed away. In our previous Spanish border crossings, local officials had seemed grim and inquisitive. On our arrival at Hendaye, however, just over the French border, no one seemed to give a hoot, and we were fairly weak with relief when we arrived safely.

Other travelers had warned us that the French were hostile to Americans. Having French friends, we didn't believe them, and France was one of our priority destinations. At the Hendaye train station's information desk, we almost changed our view.

Ticked off just a hair by the desk clerk's chilly exterior, I said to myself, "Well, dearie, if you've got the time, I'll work on it." And, miraculously, it turned out that my high school French classes had not been in vain; it began to work its way to the surface, much to Jami's astonishment. The clerk changed instantly and beamed.

Of course, I could understand only the "oui" of the rapid-fire reply, so I wasn't sure she got the message. On the platform outside I repeated my question to an attendant and got another "oui," so we chanced it, and successfully got to Toulouse, with a 24-hour stop-over in Lourdes.

Le Premier Temps

*What a lovely spring landscape that afternoon
and night in Lourdes.
Remember:
train seats and headrests
the dark tobacco smell
sudden ticket puncher
sassy Spanish rock 'n roll
views of Mediterranean villages
vineyards circling the Pyrenees
ancient nucleus inland, French farms
La Residence du Champ de Mars*

Spending time on any sort of public conveyance, nearly every day of the trip, reminded us too often that we are too short for modern train/boat/plane seat designs. That ubiquitous bump on the seat-back is probably meant to prevent neck injuries in case of an accident. If you're six feet tall I suppose it nestles soothingly under your skull, but for our 5'2" frames it never did. I suppose I didn't have to make the posture worse by wearing my hair in a bun, but even without, the angle my neck was forced to assume only hastened the development of my "dowager's hump."

Off-season though it was, all the trains we rode were crowded, and there were often no seats available. When we went from Lourdes to Toulouse, for instance, our entire car had been reserved for exuberant students returning from a ski trip in the Pyrenees. Most of them were too energetic to sit in their seats and roamed the corridor visiting each other, back and forth, keeping us standees flattened against the windows enviously eyeing their empty seats.

On my birthday in Italy two weeks later (April 28), we splurged and bought First Class tickets for a five-hour trip from Genoa to Florence, anticipating a relaxing ride along the Mediterranean coast sipping wine and munching the delectable sandwiches we'd purchased in the Genoa terminal. But it turned out there was only one car assigned to Florence, and it was second class. At least twice as many passengers boarded it as there were seats, so, having spent some time finding that particular car, we were too late for a seat. Three hours passed before we learned of the little drop seats under the windows on which we took turns. The windows didn't offer much of a view; the route went through tunnel after tunnel, with only a few brilliant flashes now and then of the beauty beyond, teasing us with peek-a-boo visions of sea and sky.

Don't get me wrong. We weren't complaining. When tempted, we'd say to each other "pinch, pinch," meaning "just think where we are—actually—not still dreaming of it."

Prior to this ride, we'd had to learn the hard way that trains are made up of cars going to different places; care must be taken to get on the right one. With so many place-names in train stations spelled in the national languages, it wasn't always easy. In my opinion,

guidebooks should use the foreign names you're going to have to decipher when abroad. We wished we'd
thought to make a list of the words for "platform" in
the various languages. Only the Portuguese and Italian
versions resemble our word, so when we were in pala-
tial stations in a new country and looking for directions
to our train, hide-and-seek was the name of the game
while quelling a certain sense of rising panic. Guidebooks rarely mention these essential names, too, and
even some dictionaries omit them. So, here's a list of
foreign equivalents of "platform" we'd have cherished,
with a few we didn't need thrown in. French: *quai*,
Spanish: *anden*, German: *bahnsteig*, Romanian: *per-
on*, Arabic: *rasif*, Czech: *nastupiste*, Greek: *exe'dra*,
Hebrew: *duchan*.

In Genoa, we ambled onto a *piattaforma*, way too
early per usual, and when we asked an attendant which
track our train would be on, he responded in a frenzy,
pulling and pushing us toward a quivering car on the

nearby track, then hoisted us bodily onto the train as it began to pull out—at least twenty minutes before its scheduled departure. It's a blessing, as in this instance, that even in small towns, helpful uniformed employees can be found near most platforms. And nearly every station offers sandwiches, baked goods, fruit, cheese, wine, and beer close to or on the platform, much of it fresh, delectable, and unique.

Every meal we had in a dining car was superb and typical of the region; course after course served with painstaking artistry, imagination, and flourish. Even the snack bars on some trains *sans* dining cars offered fresh salads and fruit; they were not always limited to plastic-wrapped, production-line sandwiches, though those did crop up now and again.

The train experience most direly affected by our language handicap happened on the Trans European Express (TEE) from Florence to Paris. In Genoa, we had

On the Portugese train. Tiny bottles of liqueurs served on a silver tray + complimentary...

learned that *biglietto* meant "ticket," so on our arrival in Florence, we proceeded to the window thus designated; it also touted *reservas*. We needed both a ticket and a reservation for the TEE. I consulted our Italian dictionary and train schedule carefully and wrote out a note that I pushed under the bars of the ticket window. The attendant there had a good laugh, then made out two large cards, wrote down the amount of lira required, and all seemed well. Off we went in search of a phone booth to call our friends, before enjoying three days of a relaxed visit, secure in the knowledge our transportation from here afterward was assured. We felt even better when our friends were surprised at how reasonably priced the long journey to Paris was. We waited a long while in a telephone booth line only to discover that this phone required tokens, not currency; then we switched to a different line for the tokens, then back to the original line for the phone. This was but one example of a public telephone requiring tokens; you can lose a good half-hour this way.

We woke up at 8:00 a.m. (time change, 9:00 a.m.) for docking in Genoa. We presented our passports to Customs, but we didn't clear. Our taxi driver worried about soldiers stopping our cab (it turned out OK.) Instead, we went to the railroad station and I thought of Dickens' Italian villa somewhere up there. Nice station—Italy. We got tickets to Firenze and had cappuccino. There was a bug in my first cup, but I braved another.

When we arrived in Firenze, we grabbed a phone booth—which took tokens only—and dropped our luggage. I tried to get Wesley and Shirley, friends from Saratoga, to meet us in 15 minutes. Half an hour later, they appeared and we were taken to great martinis and cheer in their small apartment. The Italian countryside with views of Florence. But there were water restrictions. Pressure.

The next day, we toured the Duomo, Accademia (Davido), Uffizi (after Fiesole), and Santa Croce where Dante, Michelangelo, Galileo, and Rossini are buried. We visited a church and heard an organ play, at last. We ate great pizza in Fiesole and Shirley showed us their former villa with a view of valley. We went to the "Blue Bar" for strawberries and cream and noticed a disco for kids in the basement. The teenagers were all smoking. Ghi [a friend] reminisced about her home. She also told us that school dances provide cases of wine; boys get sick and no one dances.

On Monday, Shirley drove us to Siena in the afternoon after the All-Italy handcraft show. I bought gifts and a tray that I then had to carry. I wasn't up on my Siena, excepting the marvelous church and museum, so we bought guides. The Square hosts medieval horse races on July 2 and August 16. There were wonderful ancient streets and Jami and Ghi climbed 360 steps to a tower across slanted streets. "+" marks the spot. We drank more cappuccino and ate pastries on the long drive back. We saw much, but no Leonardo!

Even though we had bought our reservations in advance, when we got on the train, we didn't have tickets! The conductor was pissed. We said, "OK, now what?" While Shirley had loaned us 10,000 lira, we *could only pay [our way] to Bologna. We dashed off, barely able to get a traveler's check cashed and hopped back on to Milano. From there, we bought tickets to Paris—$230 all told. An American from Napa helped us while his Italian wife explained our problem to the second conductor, who thought it was hilarious. Odd seating arrangement. No lunch.*

On the morning of our departure for Paris, we boarded the elegant train and found our seats: window seats that our advance purchase had blessed us with. This time the separate-seat compartments were separated from the hallway by curtains instead of sliding glass doors. The effect looked more luxurious, but the comfort level was not improved. We ogled the Italian landscape whizzing past until a conductor arrived to collect our tickets. Only ours, we were quickly apprised, were not tickets at all; they were reservations. The conductor made like a firecracker: he turned red, waved his arms and emitted short bursts and long cracklings of unintelligible sounds. We tried our best to explain our situation in sign language so ineffective that in the end we could only add an Italian shrug and look blank.

We had, of course, spent or exchanged all of our own lira, but had reluctantly agreed to accept 10,000 more from our prophetic hostess and friend who insisted we really should have more until we were well out of Italy; we could send it back when we reached Paris or London. I now produced this sum, but the angry conductor made us understand it would suffice only as far as Bologna, where the train would briefly pause without making an official stop. We also understood clearly that we would have to get off there. The train did stop in Milano, where we had friends, but at that station all we could do was look longingly out the window, unable to visit, because we were so far behind our planned schedule already; we had only one day remaining, with plans to see Paris and friends there. Embarrassed and miserable we re-gathered all our bags, crawled over the four other haughty occupants of the compartment and got to the exit just as the train stopped in Bologna.

An exchange window was in sight in the small station, and hope sprang anew. I bolted toward it just as an elderly gentleman slithered in ahead of me. While his business was leisurely attended to I waited in agony, pacing like an animal caged too long. Jami stood by our luggage at the train steps, helpless, as the train hummed with seeming impatience. When I finally reached the window, I pranced about and uttered strangling noises until the clerk caught on that the train outside was my goal, whereupon, as in a fast-action film, he sped up his task and handed me lira in exchange for one of our

traveler's checks.

Forget tickets. I ran back to the train in the nick of time; it had waited for us. We scrambled on board and stumbled across the rows of legs of our bored, unresponsive companions. Served them right: we were now streaming with perspiration in our heavy wraps.

A different conductor now appeared. I handed over the money, and he looked puzzled. We were about to try our pantomime act once more when the woman next to Jami spoke to him in Italian, punctuated with uncontrollable bursts of hilarity—our position not half that funny to us. No sooner was serenity re-established than the man next to me spoke up in perfect American English asking after our origin; he was from Napa, a town not a hundred miles from ours. Jami and I exchanged glances that said, "Where were these people when we needed them?" and the thought occurred to us that we had only been overwhelmed with helpfulness when we weren't traveling First Class.

On the train to Paris
Ham salad and wine at 2:00
Beautiful black woman in Switzerland
Italians indifferent
Hooray for France, streets, cars, pedestrians
Directions, arrows: ← ↑ 🔄

Let's return briefly to the transportation options in Florence. Our friend, Shirley, accompanied us on city buses, but I can't explain that complicated ticket arrangement. The Florentine bus system had ticket machines, without conductors. We never got it right, and spent twice as much as we needed to. Clever Italians?

Although Shirley had mastered the bus ticket system, she was still a novice at following directional signs on the narrow, twisting streets of Siena where she drove us one day.  She had no problem getting into the old section of town, but getting out again was another matter. We watched for the up-pointing arrow signs indicating "go straight ahead," but when we arrived at a roundabout (common to most European towns), the signs there weren't much help in designating which spoke of the wheel would lead us to the Florence Highway. After a turn or two around the roundabout, Shirley stopped alongside a young man to inquire the way in her fluent Italian. He responded with many accompanying gestures, then broke off to run for a bus just pulling away, calling back in Italian to the effect of "follow that bus." Then, gallantly, he hopped aboard and pushed his way to the back window from whence he directed us to the eventual escape route. Ask, we found, and you shall receive.

We told Shirley about a Portuguese taxi-driver who had driven us on a hairy twenty-mile route to a Pousada. When he'd picked us up at the railroad station and learned our destination, he'd driven us first to a tourist office in town, and even though it was after closing time, and then managed to unearth an English-speaking employee who telephoned the Pousada to check on our reservations. Only later did we savvy that he knew that the hotel was twenty miles away, that the boats there weren't running (a possibility we'd never heard of), that he'd better hang onto these dumb women and

In Sienna we found another use for our umbrella
besides keeping off rain...

get a rare good fare during this pre-season lull. Rather than resenting his opportunism, we were grateful conditions made him so eager to be helpful: a case of mutual compensation.

A few times during our 60 days abroad, boats were the only means, or the preferred means, of "getting there." On the tour, we had crossed the Guadiana River in Spain on a tiny ferry that barely contained the big tour bus, and we then rode a larger ferry from Algeciras across the Strait of Gibraltar to Tangier, on the northern tip of Morocco, without a bus.

Traveling independently, we had arranged our itinerary to proceed from Barcelona to Genoa, in Italy, hoping the dotted lines we saw on a map between these two points, across the Balearic Sea, meant we could travel by boat. But, strange as it seemed, we could not find any concrete information on this point before we left the States. The Spanish tourist office did send us a brochure in Spanish that included photos of boats and a note saying, "contact this company in June." Once we were in Barcelona, the travel agent there was able to help more specifically with actual ferry tickets, and we ventured onto our first true sea voyage. "Ferry" or no, it was the largest vessel either of us had been on, and covered the longest distance, the trip taking nearly 24 hours (if you count the hours spent waiting to shove off and then dock).

We were somewhat concerned about seasickness. Nausea, of all human ailments I've yet to experience, is most definitely the one I tolerate least, but I had done all right on the ferry across the Strait of Gibraltar (having forgotten to take the suggested pill), and decided to risk it again this time, artificial agents of control being another undesirable element. Jami, however, opted to take the pill, more to appease her imagination than her actual response to the motion. As it turned out, we both felt OK, never missing a meal; and although the sea was very rough, and we weren't quite aboard long enough to develop "sea legs," we thoroughly enjoyed watching the waves crash against the lounge windows, hearing John Wayne speak dubbed Spanish in a movie, and being rocked to sleep below.

At one point, a guy hung over our table as we played cribbage. He said something.

I answered, "*Je ne sais pas,*" telling Jami it wasn't as exciting in English.

She said, "Is 'Duh' more exact?"

We talked about the ferry's waterbeds, the merry-go-round, the icy water, sharks. We thought of its squishy seats, comfortable chairs, and glass tables.

We sweated for a minute when we saw a man in a cabin with two bunks (two more out of sight), thinking we'd paid for an outside cabin for two, and accosted the purser to clear it up. We thought we had been put in a quadruple for 4,000 lira, but had paid 5500 for a double, so we accosted a second purser. He finally made us understand that a "quad" meant four people in a cabin. We shut up, since our room was so tiny even we two couldn't move without one climbing into *the bunk.*

*Still, the porthole's extra space should mean some-
thing. Where was our guardian angel? On second
thought, we speculated it might be too bloody cold in
an outside cabin since we were just barely warm as
it was. As we sat in the lounge, Jami was concerned
about a family we were taking seats from with five
kids.*

*The sea was rough and smashed against the port
windows. A little five-year-old from an affectionate family squealed—he was showing off for me. We
closed the brown-and-white blinds, watched a Spanish movie, and napped before visiting the self-service
restaurant: paella, fish, salad, and wine. Public transportation here has terrific food. We saw the Spanish
scarf we'd searched all over Spain for in the display
case. The clerk wasn't interested—he wouldn't take
lira and we'd spent all of our pesetas. I said I could
come back in the morning, but he never reopened.*

*I found I loved the motion and didn't need to take
anti-nausea pills. It's amazing to be behind the breakers. The windows were too wet for pictures, so we
drank gin and tonics, played cribbage, and lunged.
The French Connection would be shown, but that night
we went to bed instead and slept like babies.*

I'll not soon forget that ship for another reason:
my one obsessive shopping quest in Spain had been
to find and purchase a shawl like those worn by flamenco dancers. City after city, shop after shop carried
shawls, but all I could find were large square ones with
short fringe. Yet, there in a display case in the ship's

"lobby" was the object of my pursuit, halfway to Italy. The prize remained un-won, however, and may be still carefully pinned to the back of the display case on that ship, for the purser refused to take either lira or my traveler's check, and our pesetas were long gone. He promised he'd sell me the shawl the following  morning when the ship's exchange window opened, but he did not return. I suspected he didn't want to spoil the display. Too late did it occur to me to find a theatrical supply store or to simply ask a dancer for advice.

Back to Paris: on our arrival there, we learned about the custom of waiting in line for taxis, which we later experienced in London as well. In Paris, we stood for an hour and a half after our arrival at the train station, waiting for a taxi that would take us onward. The cabs didn't all go to just any address. The waiting lines were clearly organized, and others waiting in line were, on the whole, courteous and patient.

We arrived in Paris at twelve and met our friend, Wendy. We stood in the queue for an hour and a half for a taxi; the drive was a fury and the woman at the wheel kept pointing out sights as they flashed by. Our room is adorable with flowered wallpaper tiles, a gable window, slanted closet, and quilts. A separate entry room with its own sink, shower, and bidet, with the toilette across the hall. I climbed the slanted bed and tried to get some sleep, but it was cold. The peak of the Eiffel Tower is visible from our sixth-floor window.

Upon waking, I discovered I'd goofed on the dates and that we had only one day in the city. Still, we found the bank, tabac with stamps, and pharmacie all in an adjacent block on Rue de Basque. We set out in a taxi to buy tickets via hovercraft to London before being dropped off at the Louvre to see as many paintings as possible from 11:00 a.m. to 2:00 p.m. Then we wandered through the fabulous Notre Dame and lit candles. It snowed as we took pictures by the Jeanne d'Arc statue. The stained-glass windows were unbelievable. We ate lunch across the street: Boeuf Bourguignon, mushrooms (cold), rosé, French-fried potatoes, ice cream, and coffee.

We couldn't find the church on Île St. Louis, but were shown in by a girl after asking a local. It was charming in white and gold with small simple paintings. Jack Kerouac was baptized at the St. Louis sister church in Lowell, Massachusetts. I lit a candle for him in front of Mary's statue, sat, and meditated awhile. There was only one other small group inside, and at first, I found their French annoying, but then realized it added to the effect.

The sun was shining as we walked across the bridge and took pictures of ourselves with Notre Dame in the background. The banks were closed and we were out of money, so we went back to our room to crunch *some numbers. The snow revived and we had no heat in our radiator. Seventy-year-old men and women were dressed in full mountain-climbing regalia—knee socks, boots, and backpacks—in La Land du Nord.*

On the train:

Northern French narrow tall houses
Steep-pitched roofs and gables
Variegated gingerbread trim and chimneys
Hansel and Gretel cottages in bucolic countryside
Clear dawn days, orange trees
Compartment seats open to a window
Draft down neck, stiff seats, but we
are two, facing all, alone

We had enjoyed our first long-anticipated view of Paris from a taxi window. My French wasn't good enough to know what all those interfering placards announced.

In Paris, we made no move to ride the underground. Years before in New York, both of us had vowed "never again" after only a couple of trips on that city's subway. So we can't report on that mode of transportation in Paris. But later in London, poor planning forced us to brave the tube near the last week of our stay and we fell in love, wishing we'd discovered the pleasure sooner. What a contrast to our former experiences in the

States. Here the underground was efficient, clean and orderly; the people considerate, helpful and patient; the stops' walls covered with displays of varied décor, from mere advertising (fun for us Americans), to highly artistic murals.

A hovercraft (or, more romantically in French, an *aéroglisseur*) was by far the most unique method of getting from here to there that we utilized, from Calais, France, to Dover, England. On this craft, we sat near a group of volatile and vocal French girls who had also shared our train compartment from Paris to Calais. For five days we'd heard only French and the girls' incessant chatter for the preceding many hours, so on the English train, when a lunch cart came near us and we prepared to buy sandwiches and wine, Jami turned to me in a panic, and said,

"How do I say, 'How much?'"

"You say, 'How much?'" I replied, "We're in England now."

When we noticed a British couple across the aisle, there could be no further doubt. The man, a typical British bloke in coordinated checkered tweeds, was reading a book entitled *Memoirs of a Fox-Hunting Man*. Welcome to England! In a movie such a scene might be considered too corny or obvious, what with Mum pouring tea from a thermos and passing the cheese, oatcakes, and apples. We ate our lunch and sipped our wine per usual from the little gold and silver cups we'd obtained at Lourdes that were meant to carry healing waters. At first, we'd been hesitant to use them thusly, wondering if the practice might be sacrilegious, before we

remembered that Jesus, too, had exchanged water for wine.

After a few days of wallowing in London using every kind of conveyance with pleasure, we bought a Coach Pass, and an "Open to View" pass, and set out to explore the country. It was a bank holiday, and we assumed that meant the banks were closed. Again, it seemed no guidebook had considered anyone as ignorant as we, as we learned for ourselves that very few Coaches run on bank holidays, and tours and tourist attractions are mostly shut up tight.

We checked into the Alison House Hotel and went to a picturesque pub, but it was too full of loud rock 'n roll. We ate at The Tent before bed, which was excellent, but $12. On Friday morning, we got "Coach Master Pass" bus tickets at Victoria station and signed up for a two-hour tour to fit in before visiting Queen's Gallery, the National Gallery, Trafalgar Square, the National Portrait Gallery, the British Museum—King

Edward VIII—and Great Russell Street. Called Jay.

My interview for Honey Magazine *was scheduled for 7:30 p.m. with Minty. Wine shop across the street—had bought wine already, but didn't have dinner.*

Saturday Itinerary

Buckingham Palace, Changing of the Guard,
Victoria and Albert Museum
Treasures of Prints Room
Royal Portrait Gallery
Hampton Court
Costume Museum
Art and flowers
Chapter House
Westminster Abbey
Eat. Tea and wine at Landesman's (Stewart
        Hogarth).
"The Crucible of Blood" at Haymarket
"The Mousetrap" at St. Martins

We walked to Sherlock Holmes' Baker Street and talked to a waitress at the Duke of Buckingham Pub, which had lovely antique décor. American rock 'n roll played as the bitters, ale, and gin settled in. Hot, stuffy, noisy, friendly.

We met a great guide on a Charles Dickens walking tour who stood on tiptoes. Embankment Underground: saw river gate place where a blocking factory was (it never moved), rookeries, arches to which Dickens referred in his books... Duke of Buckingham's palace. Then to Adelphi section: buildings still there—Pepys' home—houses with torch snuffers, more rookeries and slums. Went to Rules Restaurant (36 Maiden Lane) where Dickens went. Saw Peabody's slum clearance buildings. We were thrilled to finally see Covent Garden, home of our favorite ballet company, The Royal Ballet. Noted Adam's architecture where buildings appear laced at the seams.

At a late opera gala, Prince Michael of Kent (the Queen's nephew) sat close to us during dress rehearsal. It was a wonderful show, though we waited for the prince for an hour and a half outside, hoping to catch a ride. We then couldn't get a cab and more than two hours passed before we decided to just walk home. We spotted the Prince's car at Buckingham Palace. We had a "pint" of bitters in the Duke of Edinburgh Pub where a nice young man explained the mug he was holding, but I couldn't hear, and coughed until 4:30 a.m.

We were on the trail of Dickens and other literary greats and wanted a bus schedule for southern routes; our first stop was to be Gravesend, according to the map previously consulted. Hi ho, the merry morons queued up at the Information Center at Victoria Station at 10:00 a.m. on a Sunday, the day before our planned departure—and the bank holiday. The Information girl told us to go to the Victoria Coach Station (later in the week we would come to fully understand the distinction that "buses" are local and "coaches" long distance). Once there, we queued up again and eventually got our chance to request a bus schedule. We were informed that "those schedules are the size of phone books; we don't give them out," and were directed to the Green Line Coach Station. We walked there and queued up, and were eventually told, "There are no coaches to Gravesend, only to Rochester. The train goes to Gravesend." Back, then, to the Victoria (train) Station where we queued up at the train ticket window. There, we learned that we were at the "wrong station. That train leaves from Charing Cross." Having already worn a comfortable groove in the few blocks between stations, we decided to skip Gravesend this trip and go to Rochester instead. Back, then, to the Green Line and another queue. "No," was the response to our request there, "Rochester's too far for the Green Line; go [back] to the Victoria Coach Station." There we queued first for tickets and then again for seat reservations. After an hour and a half, the job was done.

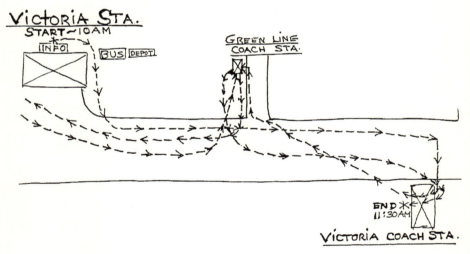

We queued up for the reservation window and finally got the seats and passes validated—eureka! It had taken one and a half hours to do this tour. No fish and chips yet.

Sign on every street corner: "LOOK RIGHT →"

Next time, we'll stay put on a bank holiday; but we still don't know how travel is completed on other days.

The next morning, we got on the bus—er, coach—at the Victoria Train Station for Rochester, where we were richly compensated with Dickens' mementos in spite of many shops being closed. It didn't take long to see what there was to see, so we continued our journey on local buses, as there were no more coaches running from Rochester.

On to Faversham: Everything was closed up tight, though people were in the streets. We saw a block of buildings in mid-street and a central well with pink paint and the Tudor rose on it. Charming town.

Then on to Canterbury by back roads—lovely farms. We got there at 5:00, but it had taken all day to drive 50 miles. We arranged for a bus to Rye the next day, and walked down its main street of old Elizabethan buildings and Roman remains (exhausted), and passed through a great wall to a gate that the bus had to squeeze through. The tourist office was closed, but we turned back just as a man was leaving, so he went back in to call some hotels for us: no baths.

Finally, we stayed at the County Hotel, four stars and a nice downstairs room, bath, and color TV. But it had a tacky color and thin towels with cheap bedding (Woolworth's) but Oh Joy, we washed in the tub just before the radiator cooled. We went out for groceries but all had already closed, so I had a horrible sandwich. There was no service in the coffee shop or in the hotel.

But then delicious bath, Harvey Cream and ten hours of sleep and rarin' to go in the morning. We saw a cathedral, shopped, packed, and got the bus at 12:10 p.m. Beautiful countryside surrounded wealthy old manor houses and picture-book farms.

In Ashford, the bus station girl said, "You're lucky. The bus to Rye only runs on Tuesday at 2:10 p.m.," and it was only 1:00 p.m.! It was a clean, large town with a brand-new-looking Norman church, but Jami complained of no entertainment.

We had a lunch of steak and mushroom pie with chips (great French fries) for only £3.24. No salads, "too expensive." We caught the crowded bus to Rye; I'd have missed it if Jami hadn't been watching the other way. There was a survey for bus service on board and when I began writing comments, a lady behind me said, "Hun, you don't have to write a ten-page article, you know," but in a very jolly tone. Everyone in England is friendly and sweet.

Canterbury Cathedral was surrounded with fresh flowers and the same atmosphere of love and care as Rochester. Repair work in progress: dreadful destruction, an exhibit being built in the crypt—to think it survived the bombs—and new stained-glass windows with Disney-like faces that were too garish. Other windows were exquisite.

Thus initiated one of our happiest memories of Britain, a series of bus trips through the "garden of England" and along the coast; wherever the double-decker buses took us, we enjoyed views of beautiful countryside in its Spring array; and chatted with

schoolchildren, their parents, their hamsters—English folk of all sorts—with growing admiration. All the drivers and conductors we encountered on those buses were patient and congenial, calling everyone "luv" or "dearie," and delaying the bus's progress to give detailed directions to lost souls. One even stopped the bus in open country to let a mother take her small child to a nearby bush. The passengers on those trips were equally patient and cheerful, accepting our presence with friendly condescension, probably wondering why we had so much baggage on a local run.

The back road to Rye was full of brick houses, sheep, lambs, cattle, fabulous country homes, and ever-blooming tended gardens. The fruit orchards in Kent were all in bloom, too. Next was Appledore, a neat, beautiful little village with sheep, geese, and immaculate hedges. Sunny day, warm with a cool breeze, fields of flowers and a creek with fish.

We took the long way 'round to Rye, which was great! There were country lanes with Norman or Saxon churches, and the railroad gates were opened and closed by hand. But Rumer [a friend] no longer lives in Lamb House and unfortunately for us too, it isn't open on Tuesdays, so we boarded a different bus to Eastborne and then to Brighton. I'm learning we have not been inquiring about "coaches," the express service. I happened to see a bus change its sign and so we got on half an hour early, but it then turned around and faced the other way. We'd never have even seen it had I not happened to look at that moment. So, then we weren't meant to see this ancient and fascinating town. Others await.

We took a double-decker bus to Icklesham and saw an incredible farm house with a brick cottage with a garden, dog, and sheep at the gate. I think the windmills signal a Dutch influence and it was the most beautiful yet with country homes right out of a movie. We glanced a bus-load of schoolchildren from Rye to Hastings, the bay, a watch tower, and briefly saw a huge Norman castle in the glen. Hastings had rows of uniform brick houses on one side of the hill that were painted on their back sides; "public conveniences" that were crowded; old intermingled churches; pot-bellied Tudor shops; a fort overlooking the bay; and a touristy waterfront. It was a bit grimy on first view without the charm of Rye, but we didn't have time to explore. Still, there was a clean rock beach for a big city. Sign: "Have you paid and displayed" in the parking lot.

Scaffolds are everywhere and the bus stops at every other pole. There was a pleasure palace built out over the water and we saw shops, restaurants, dancing, white-washed domes, and little towers. There were rows of houses facing long meadows with steps to the sea and other bunches of houses on the beach. Are they watchtowers in those back yards or storage tanks? Converted? The seaside country, clean roadsides, and well-kept farms are beyond belief.

[Little did Carolyn and Jami guess that Carolyn would move to this area four years later. In 1983, she sold the family home in Los Gatos and moved to Winchelsea, a quaint village between Hastings and Rye.]

On the way to Brighton, the bus stopped and waited to let a child use the toilet on the side of the road, so we arrived at six when everything had already closed. We were given coach times for tomorrow, since there were no more for today. (We asked if we could get any farther tonight and he suggested taking a bus to Worthing.) We did see the Royal Pavilion: not as expected. It's a faint dot on the map, so we prepared ourselves by observing houses along the waterfront as we moved along in the sunset.

We were sure Worthing would be asleep by the time we got there. We also had to pay. A young conductor explained that only some bus lines were covered by our passes and showed us [which ones] in our brochures. Well, it was only £_____. He was very helpful in pointing out closed coach offices and, much to our delight, a lovely square nearby surrounded by hotels. Of course, we aimed for the three-star (highest) and got another luxury room and bath for £22 (or that many dollars)—sigh. We had sandwiches and wine in our room, but yet another toilet had to be pumped and the "hot" and "cold" water faucets in both the sink and the shower did not work.

The next morning, we were early to the station after kippers, sausage, and poached eggs for breakfast (included in room rate). A nice lady gave us contrary information to the man in Brighton: the coach was so slow, but we had to take it and pay £2 for the bus! We sat by the sea and watched fishermen clean fish in front of customers who came along to buy right out of the boat Danny Boy. Next, we passed Arundel, but the castle was too remote to even photograph—too bad. Then we passed Holiday Park, which had a great complex of garishly painted stucco, pools, fountains, and white and blue tiles like in the TV movie we saw in Canterbury.

There was a little girl on the bus who looked like Cathy as a child, with blue eyes and freckles.

She wordlessly showed me her doll and pointed to a button pinned to her sweater, "I am four years old."

As she and her mummy were leaving, the mum said, "Be careful, you're only wee. Go very straight. That's a big girl."

There were archaeological digs here and there, though not in darling Chichester, where the fruit trees *were heavily pregnant with bloom. There was a neat arched round thing in the middle of the street by Woolworth's, or "Woolies." The cathedral is being restored, but almost too late. The houses are all named, and one is called Noglands.*

When we arrived in Portsmouth, the bus driver tried to tell us where to go.

He stopped at a street stop, and said, "Ask the bobby out there."

We asked for the coach station.

He, in his shirtsleeves, said, "Just under the RR, turn left, and it's just there, at the end of that street. It's a beautiful day for a walk..."

"Yes, but—" we started to say, but continued on, lugging our suitcases. After going several blocks to an underpass, we turned left and, in the distance, was some sort of building. We lugged on. But when a cab came, we hailed it. It must have been at least a mile, that "lovely walk."

It took us three days to get to Portsmouth—a mere forty minutes from London by train—via these local buses; but the rides made us wish we could explore the entirety of the British Isles in that fashion. Whenever darkness fell, we'd get off a bus with directions from the driver and find a bed for the night.

We finally found the Info Center for National Coaches; it was well-manned or, womaned. A nice gal went over every coach schedule with us, but there would be no way to catch one unless we spent the night.

"Try a train," she suggested.

So, we went to the train station—only a couple of blocks' walk—but Jami wanted to get a taxi to the Tourist Info Center to get the route mapped first. We hailed one and were driven across town to the Sealink and Ferry Terminal, but the kiosk office was closed and wouldn't reopen for an hour.

We got another taxi to Dickens' house and were left alone since no one else was there. Four rooms were open and refurnished. The room he was born in had definite vibrations: others have "felt a presence," said the caretaker. In the bedroom opposite, there are cases of his desk things, letters, jewelry, drawings by the illustrators, a chair of his, and the chaise he died on—un-roped off. Jami took pictures of me on it. I felt no vibes there like I had in his bedroom.

The first floor had a living room and a dining room with too-new paint and crystal mixed in with antiques, but it was otherwise tasteful. We couldn't go to the third floor, but it was fantastic nonetheless. There are houses next to it that are still lived in.

When we were going to call for a cab, the caretaker said, "What? Why the ferry station is just through there. Take this footpath to the main road and it is right there." We walked another mile, marveling at the hardy folk, and got to the Info Center at 1:05 p.m.—still closed. While we waited, we ordered beer and salad plates. The clerk arrived at 1:30 and perused the schedules, informing us that the chief Info Office was at the train/bus station we'd just taken the cab from, and found that there was no way to get to Stratford except by train through London. We gave up.

We took a cab back to the railroad station, bought tickets—this time to Waterloo for $26 more—left Portsmouth at 2:53 p.m., and arrived in London at 4:27 p.m. We found a bus to Bradford—full—but persevered and hailed a taxi to Nottingham with an arrival of 9:30 p.m. It was a lovely, warm, and sunny day. A Jamaican cab driver took us to the RR station, but an impatient clerk (all have been handsome) was not encouraging, so we asked a female constable (so many dozens of bobbies arrived as a football game let out) and she recommended the Victoria Hotel. The hotels by the RR station looked weird, but old and formerly elegant in a crummy part of town. Victoria was elegant—and another £23. It had a large double bed and a single; heating; a color TV; and a farmhouse breakfast of eggs, juice, fruit, bread, bacon, sausage, and black pudding. Good coffee. We took rolls.

Nottingham was huge and grim, and it rained this morning. Beyond the bus station next door: old stone mansions and behind those, stone ruins, terraces, and more forest—pines. Sign for a social club in a cinema building read "Eyes...down" and the time the show started. Poor viewing today: more grimy brick-stone houses, windows fogged up inside, and everything wet from Mansfield to Sheffield. I read a biography of Emily Dickinson en route to the next few towns.

The local bus daisy-chain pushing us two days behind our planned schedule, we had to sacrifice the West of England and push off for the North. Because of the unseasonal weather there, too, not only were many establishments not open, but fewer buses and trains were running, so we spent a good deal of time hanging about, as we'd done in Portugal. A car would have been jolly helpful in these instances, but we'd have missed all the lovely people.

Over time, it became apparent that our Coach Pass was good on some buses but not others. Once, when we thought it was valid when it wasn't, our young conductor said, "never mind, luv; forget it," not wanting to bother us for the fare. We came up with it anyway, and tried to imagine that happening in the good old U.S. of A.

We spread out in the back seats of local buses and pressed on. Our passes weren't as good, but perseverance continued. We changed at Sheffield, which was full of outdoor sheds, but the cafeteria had great food and it was clean and warm. The bus stations are not like ours: few loiterers, if any, and everyone is so cheery and kind, though they look sour until spoken to. We get called "dearie," "luv," or "darlin'" everywhere we go.

In Britain, we had no meals on the vehicles themselves, but we were astonished by the excellent food available in bus stations and "tea stops," no matter how remote or humble. And that made us mightily ashamed of what foreign visitors to America have to endure in our bus and train stations—not only in terms of food.

Scrapbook References

For Morocco, see Page 46

For Portugal, see Page 3

For Hella, the tour guide, see Page 29

For the gala dinner, see Page 2

For the Diplomático, see Page 69

For the Altis, see Page 64

For the Aveiro, see page 71

For Oporto, see Page 72-74

For Barcelona, see Pages 84-94

For San Sebastian, see Page 75

For Hendaye, see Page 76

For Lourdes, see Pages 77-79

For the tickets from Genoa to Florence, see Page 76

For the train trip from Florence to Paris, see Page 76

For Italy tour, see Pages 96-103

For the ferry across the Strait of Gibraltar, see Pages 46-51

For map of trip from Spain to Italy, see Page 76

For Paris, see Pages 105-111

For Île St. Louis (Church), see Page 110

For Notre Dame, see Pages 108-109

For the hovercraft, see Page 112

For London, see Pages 113-121

For Alison House Hotel, see Pages 113-114

For Dickens tour in London, see Page 123, 127

For Faversham, see Pages 124-125

For the "Garden of England," see Pages 126-127

For Portsmouth, see Page 122 (map)

For Carolyn at the Dickens house, see Page 127

For Victoria Hotel, see Page 128

TWO

"The Body in Question"

PERHAPS MANY OF US have been lured by glories seen in travel films or location backdrops in movies. Well, there's a stupendous difference between two dimensions and three. Being there in the flesh, we have to take our bodies along. Eyeballing a place or vista may seem like it would be much the same as seeing it on a screen, but our other senses and organs clamor to be part of the experience, sometimes adding bright new dimensions of satisfaction, at other times unanticipated and annoying demands. Tasting, smelling, hearing, and touching new and different stimuli contributed tremendously to the thrill of the discoveries and to our memories thereof. Even a bed or a bath can be long-remembered as a definite plus. Then again, physical discomfort can turn what might have been a plus to a minus.

Beds, for example: near the coast of Portugal, our hotel's bed sheets were unavoidably clammy and cold.

We would open wide our bedding before going to dinner to attempt to dry it out. Invariably though, a maid would have the beds again all tidy and tight upon our return. In Spain, where the beds tended to be dry, we liked lounging on them or using them for repacking. But early in the evening, maids would appear, bent on turning them down. In Madrid, we had to insist, almost as defiantly as this:

Eventually we learned to put our "Do Not Disturb" sign on the room door the minute we arrived. Somehow, we'd survived this long without help getting into bed—even if we weren't accustomed to two bedspreads on every bed. Pillows on twin beds were the width of the bed, flat and hard, or very loosely-filled; occasionally we each got one apiece.

Other than a few three-day stopovers, we spent every night of our 60-day trip in a different unique hotel room, from palaces, both ancient and modern, to cabins and attic rooms, and we loved playing house in them all. The tour accommodations were diverse, and we appreciated the variety. On our own, we followed the same guidelines, sometimes finding charming bargains, sometimes splurging with the money we'd saved from those. Even if we could have toted the appropriate wardrobe, we still wouldn't have cared about top-drawer extravagance or prestigious addresses.

In Albufeira, Portugal we found a super new high-rise hotel—450 rooms—far from the village and beach. We drove through fig and orange orchards on an old country road to get to the manor, a severe white thing. Hove into the one-year old mammoth Montechoro Hotel where Hella had been the first guest. She told us of the electricity failure there, how the elevators quit earlier, and that the baggage didn't arrive. The dining room is like a mess hall, huge and noisy with no atmosphere. The water pressure varies as does the hot water. One sink stopped up. Toilet seat of cheapest plastic. In another year, it'll be a slum.

Our room is large and sparsely furnished in a modern style with a glass table and overstuffed chairs in white, grey, and fuchsia. But the marble-topped bath with two basins isn't working. There's a flimsy shower curtain to no effect. One ashtray in the whole place, one crooked picture in the hallway next to older master drawings: bits of Bosch beautifully framed, either antique or copies. Ultra-modern steel lights frame the beds. The balcony has a white wall and white, plastic chairs. It would have been good for sunbathing if it hadn't been raining, though I suspected it would be hot and the view obscured. Cheap; not the Ritz. The room was the biggest, but without charm, no "home."

I'm complaining? Well, by now we're spoiled. I criticize taste and motives. Again, the plumbing is a catastrophic noise! We took pictures off the balcony, even though surrounded by fog.

Later, we saw Maggie Cassidy *on an English book rack outside a café in Faro where Hella made a stop earlier to show us the square and the harbor. Lots of young internationals.*

Meals

Three times a day
plus two breaks eating with others we're
forced into conversation with, there's interest,
but three to five days of this?
We can't wait to eat and get on
Each meal
Modern light switches

I resent this plastic monument to greed defacing the charming village. Below us are new structures quite in keeping with the original of the town; this has been possible since the revolution. Hotel full of families and darling children.

Breakfast was a sick display of cold cuts and dubious fruits. No oranges. There were dozens of waiters, but it took forever to get coffee. Pastries inferior. Hella informed us that the Sun City diplomat, Hazel, is ill with dysentery.

We were bundled up when our bus arrived in the village, since it showered earlier. We left our wash on the balcony, and in town the sun came out as we weaved our way aimlessly through the narrow, cobbled streets among other tourists until I bought a book with a map. It was difficult to figure out, but we followed it to a recommended "rustic" restaurant, though the rest of the group wanted a more elegant one.

Winding, climbing, plunging little streets with the sidewalks a foot wide. Tiny cars and motorcycles zipping along the small street. We persevered up, around, and down and found the Ruína Restaurant five minutes before it opened. The bar on the upper level had a balcony overlooking the bay and the beach was jammed with fishing boats, fishermen, fish drying in sun, trucks, and nets. We were directed down a long, curving flight of stairs to the restaurant.

There, a double-decker case held all kinds of raw fish; on top were salads, fried fish, and shrimp. There was also an enormous pot of steaming bouillabaisse. We picked our own fish, which the attendant then took out and over to the cook at the next counter who sliced it open and put it on the grill. Jami and I chose tuna salads replete with vegetables, lettuce, and the bouillabaisse, longingly eyeing the clams, sardines, sole, and bass.

But our choice was too filling anyway what with the wine and fresh grainy bread—best we've had: both the salad dressing and the soup needed mopping with it. Every kind of fish. The bouillabaisse: whole sardines and great chunks of the others, plus vegetables, completely satisfying. The Atlantic crashed on the beach below.

Hella appeared, meeting Phillipe and his son, who turned out to be tall and mustached! We went to the bar terrace to drink port outside—perfectly lovely. Our only disappointment was our determination to speak Portuguese, but everyone spoke English! After baking ourselves, we walked down narrow steps to the beach and among the boats, picked up rocks and shells, and smiled at the charging water. Later, back up and into the narrow, bumpy streets and down into the square, we bought oranges at the market; wine, cheese, chocolate, and yogurt in the grocery store. A big bottle of sparkling Lancers cost 96 escudos, or two dollars.

We hopped back on the bus hoping to sunbathe at the hotel, but our balcony was covered in shade. Still, our clothes were dry and safe. We also bought stamps at the post office—a store open during siesta! A lovely, lovely day. Wonderful people. Jami and I played cribbage and napped without a schedule. During the bus ride, our friend Sue said she didn't like this town too much and hated places catering to tourists. Jami and I laughed together because Sue only wanted to shop and loved the big shopping places—a total tourist. She bought three tablecloths here (ugh) whereas Jami and I always tried to avoid shops and the tourists.

The room was like a hospital one, but we were happy. The music on the radio was a mixture of everything, with a little too much American rock or funk.

Sagres

The Lighthouse is the sleeping place of the
    goddesses
No one dared go at night
We climbed to the prism, two bulbs
3,000 watts, 60 miles for airplanes
Protected courtyards, no plants, warm São
    Vicente
Southwest corner of Europe, Henrique the
Navigator
spent forty years at the fort
Phillipe is driving fast
Primary school cupola

One most welcome difference from the U.S., was our discovery that in European hotels—which tend to have no need to fear vandals or thieves—one could enjoy well-made often antique furnishings, beautiful drawings, paintings and sculpture, and locally-produced crafts. You are made to feel you really are a guest.

Many European hotel rooms contain a compact refrigerator-bar stocked with small bottles of a large variety of drinks, both alcoholic and soft, plus snacks and ice—and they have for the past fifteen or twenty years, yet we had read not one word in reference to them. We've since learned a few places in the U.S. are trying them out, but likely fearing dishonesty among patrons. We thought it a great idea; one can kick off her shoes and relax while resting, dressing or bathing, with no need to call for expensive room-service. In Spain, the two times we found a refrigerator-bar in our room, the management certainly had no fear of vandals—nor indeed, any expectation of even getting paid, for the doors were unlocked with no way to tally what we (and the maids?) consumed. We can't tell you how they're supposed to work.

And why did no one mention how tiny and often creaky hotel elevators are throughout Europe? They did nothing to smooth our chicken feathers.

It was a relief to find that stamps could be purchased at hotel desks, and even if the desk clerks often didn't understand English too well, sign language is a cinch for stamp needs. In Spain, the price changed almost daily, and each letter required several, but despite feeling unsure that we got it right every time, all the letters and cards we sent arrived where they should.

While on the tour, we spent an entire afternoon and evening at the extraordinary Bussaco Palace in Portugal, high on a forested hill. The weather, per the trip's usual, was cold and grey, so after a brief inspection of the grounds, many of us used the time to catch up on our reports to our near and dear at home, snuggling ourselves in cozy Palace parlors in front of ornate fireplaces, toasting our toes and our good fortune from a self-serve tea cart. In the entrance hall, when we asked the concierge for stamps, he replied, "Give me your

mail, and I will put them on for you," which he did with
paste and a brush.

We had been told we could purchase Aerograms
at tobacco shops in Spain. The first time we tried to,
we couldn't get the girl at the counter to understand
what we wanted. We thought we performed wonderful
pantomime, and I drew a number of sketches to clarify
further. Although she brought out everything she had
from drawers and under the counter, she didn't produce an Aerogram. A soldier came in midway through
the attempt, and after watching our antics for a minute,
he told the girl what we were looking for in Spanish. She
didn't have any. Still trusting, we continued the search
at every stop, but only when we got to England could
we find them. Then, of course, we bought too many.

One of the guidebooks we'd consulted before leaving had suggested setting an average daily fixed expen-
diture goal. We tried it and found it worked very well.

We derived extra pleasure from both savings and compensatory extras.

We had joined the Hostel Club before leaving home and had anticipated extending our budget by staying at hostels whenever convenient, but with the tiring pace, the unusual cold wet weather, and our respiratory problems, we decided against that sort of adventure. A hot bath and warm room were mandatory to keep us going. We walked everywhere we could, and not only were our hotels invariably either at the top or bottom of steep hills, we seemed singled out to occupy rooms on the top floors as well ("I'm sorry there's no lift; they won't let me take out this beautiful stairway").

We arrived in Barcelona during a convention and were told by all the tourist centers we could find that there were no vacant rooms in the city. We knew this couldn't be true. We scoured the Ramblas area downtown, where we wanted to settle. After about five rejections, the sixth concierge said, "Yes, we have a room, but it's _____ pesetas," a sum nearly twice our daily budget. Meekly, we took it. It was clean enough, but it appeared to be the catch-all for leftover bedspreads, draperies and furniture; nothing matched in color or design, and no effort appeared to have been expended on charm. We did not exactly feel spoiled.

We told ourselves that unless we could find a less expensive room, we'd have to leave this city we'd so looked forward to visiting. The next morning, we walked across the street and checked into the Monte Carlo for half the price and ten times the charm, a room with a bay window and balcony overlooking the Ramblas area, and loaded with imaginative Spanish handiwork in brilliant red and gold, blue and silver, plus handwoven spreads.

Throughout Britain, we generally found the Tourist Information Centers well organized and efficient, but for some reason they kept booking us into the most remote and dreary accommodations that could provide our one steadfast request: both a tub and a shower. We couldn't always succeed in finding rooms that fit the bill within our budget. And, often, the bathroom was a short hike from the room, and the town's point of interest a long one.

In Oban, Scotland, a man on a bus kindly recommended a room in a grim little street adjacent to the bus and train depots. We thanked him and headed instead for a posh hotel in the opposite direction beside Oban Bay. The desk clerk gave us a fishy once-over and said the rooms were fully booked. A gentleman lounging on the counter said he knew of a place, led us outside, and directed us to the same roadside attraction as the bus passenger had. We persisted on our own, and found a room overlooking the Bay in another grand old hotel, whose personnel were more perceptive, with what seemed a little more trust—not based solely on appearances.

In Edinburgh, the Information Center booked us into a top floor garret in a remodeled home on a street of identical grey buildings three or four blocks below Princes Street at the bottom of a steep hill. In York, England, we were once again directed to a small place a long way from the sights, but this time we were wiser and looked around ourselves before committing to their

choice. We headed for the Minster, and on the corner directly facing it was Dean's Inn. Our room was in the front and, lying on our beds, we looked up into stained glass and stone tracery, illuminated at night. This, we knew, would not be available at home.

The fact that the bathrooms abroad differ greatly from most standard ones in the U.S. was not once mentioned in any of the literature we read, nor by our friends. These accommodations not only differ in general from stateside examples, but also vary widely from one another.

Never had we suspected there were so many ways to flush a toilet, (though along the Iberian Way many of them didn't flush at all). Illustrated are but a few of the more common varieties I can remember. At the flamenco club we attended in Barcelona, I searched in vain for something to push, pull, turn or step on. At the door were two light switches side-by-side, but I could see only one light fixture. I took a chance and flicked them both. Olé!

No one had cared to mention, either, that it takes at least four turns to get a European faucet to spout, and everywhere, even in the newest hotels, the noise of all the plumbing functions during or long after use raises fear that the pipes are connected to the bowels of the earth, are hollow, and ready to erupt in untapped volcanoes.

We had heard a lot of grumbling about European bathrooms over the years from returning travelers, so we were not surprised by the stretchy, dyed (puce, green or lavender) crêpe toilet paper found in outlying areas. It wasn't our favorite, either, and we could never acquire the knack (if there is one) of tearing the unperforated surface on the dull-edged lids encasing the rolls. The transparent slick stuff is far worse than the crêpe. Most newer public bathrooms and all the private ones had very satisfactory toilet paper, though one often had to rent the roll from an attendant or use your own Kleenex. We had rather a queer feeling using the paper in British galleries and museums, where

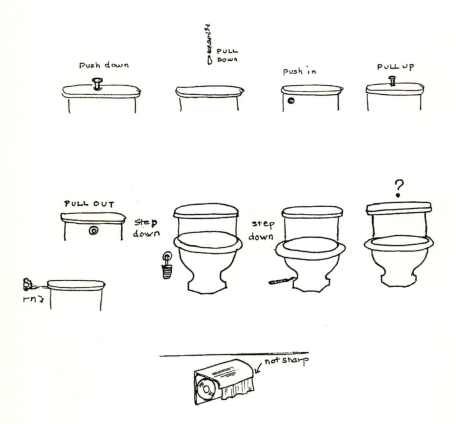

each square was stamped "Government Property." Said property was, necessarily, defaced and destroyed at a rapid rate—which is of course against the law here at home.

Now, of course, I'd known about bidets for most of my life, but since we'd not read or heard mention of them recently, I'd not thought about them for years, so at our first encounter with a shiny new one we decided it had a much more useful function than a conventional one.

And why had no one thought it of interest to mention that most European bathtubs are enormous? Many of them are six feet long and nearly two feet deep. And, that bath towels are huge, soft, thick and snowy white?

Our familiar H and C were missing from faucets, replaced by international red and blue dots—akin to the walking figures on stoplights that consider all nationalities. Then, too, there was the ubiquitous cord hanging on the wall behind the tub. They were ever-present, but we felt too timid to ask after their purpose, too chicken to pull one and find out. Maybe it's to summon someone

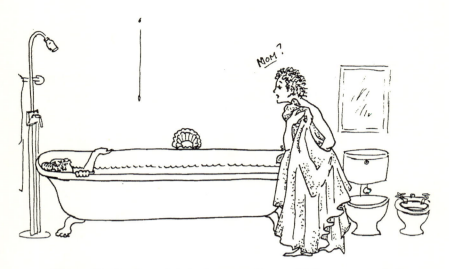

if you slip in the tub? Or in case the maid forgot towels?
Bolder travelers will have to answer that one.

In contrast, on our first rest stop along the road
in Portugal, the co-ed toilet was separated from the
snack bar by only about four feet of floor space and
a flimsy curtain. By that point, we didn't care at all,
but we were glad to move
on, out of nasal range.

Plumbers on the other
side of the Atlantic seem not
to have mastered the tech-
nique of channeling hot and
cold water through one pipe.
If you want warm water, you
have to fill the basin with
both. Showers, although
delivering water through
a single shower head, tend
to alternate blasts of hot
and cold water, keeping
one hopping. In our tiny

London so-called hotel, the advertised promise "with bath" turned out to mean prefabricated shower stalls crammed into the narrow staircase landings between floors. There were no tubs. The window in our room couldn't be closed, nor the heater activated, even after it gobbled up the required 25 pence. The hardy British.

Let's get out of the bathrooms and into dining rooms. Although food is a subject covered in detail in most travel books, we had not read or heard that throughout Europe only sweet butter would be served, and only white pepper. A tenacious myth we had heard prior to leaving was that "the Spanish don't know how to cook vegetables and rarely serve salads." Balderdash. We enjoyed a variety of fresh, al dente vegetables there, some covered in heavenly sauces, alongside both lunch and dinner, as well as salads equal to or surpassing the standard U.S. "dinner salad" in size and quality, with the added delight of watercress sprouts.

Since most of the U.S. promotional material encouraging Spanish travel could lead one to think of Spain as hot and dry like Andalusia, we had vaguely expected spicy food there, similar to Mexican cuisine. Also, we had heard or read over and over that Portuguese and Spanish food is swimming in olive oil and garlic. Not once did we have such a dish, nor could we identify any one typical Spanish dish, not even paella, a variation of which is served in every coast town. Although an Arabic influence is occasionally apparent, Spanish cuisine is generally "European." Even a truly "Spanish omelet" contains only potatoes among the eggs, and bears no resemblance (aside from the eggs) to its Western American counterpart. And the Iberians do wonders with potatoes, a vegetable we had not expected to find there, but which was served at both lunch and dinner in infinite varieties. The "French" fries were superb.

Fresh fruit was available at every meal; we'd never seen this in the U.S. outside of elaborate buffets.

Sometimes it was served as a "fruit cocktail" or piled *au natural* in big bowls from which one could help oneself. Oranges at home in California never tasted as good as they did in Iberia, and we stashed extras in our pockets and bags for a wake-up treat every day. An ice-cold orange sliced in decorative shapes was a popular dessert. We were intrigued to learn that marmalade, which the English are famous for, is often made from Spanish bitter oranges. (Perhaps similarly, we watched as raw marble from Spain was loaded onto our ferry from Barcelona to Genoa, Italy, presumably to be processed and passed off as "Italian Marble" alongside the real deal.)

We knew about Continental breakfasts but had not realized how much sugar Europeans consume in the morning. And the only protein in the breakfasts we had was in the milk that went into the coffee or tea. We ate only white flour in breads, rolls and pastries, and when sugar didn't already adorn them, there were always jams and jellies. Spain offered its own unique brand of poison for breakfast: irresistible deep-fried bread rings called "churros" that add fat to the sugar. Fruit juice was available along with the fresh fruit, and we felt we took in quite enough sugar from this source.

During the tour, guides had made eggs and ham or bacon available for breakfasts on the Continent, but their quality wasn't always reliable. Soft-boiled eggs were often raw, as was the bacon. Fried eggs were usually hard and crisp. In England, on the other hand, breakfasts laden with protein outdid ours in the U.S., and often included items we knew nothing about, at least for breakfast, such as black bread, fried and baked beans, and choices of far greater variety than are customary here. And: all included in the price of your room.

In Iberia, aside from breakfast, coffee is only served after the meal, not with it. Riots might ensue if you insist on having it "with." If you persist in carrying your own country's habits with you, and don't care for café con leche, con laite or *ou lait*, the wait staff will bring you either aqua caliente (hot water) or café Americano (already thinned). We loved the rich, thick coffee with milk in every country, and it got us through mornings of cold, brisk walking, since we avoided the sugar and white breads of breakfast time.

Rarely were platefuls of food set before us as they are in America. Lunch and dinner (or dinner and supper) often consisted of five separate courses—at a minimum, with huge portions of each one—which required two hours to finish. If you can stand to miss any, you can skip a course, but we rarely did, being so eager to sample all the new tastes and textures. We resigned ourselves to becoming blimps, but we didn't gain a pound, undoubtedly offset by the miles of hills and steps we covered on foot. We concluded that the whole continent was vertical.

Each and every meal was a production, even throughout every class of the trains and boats. Each dish was presented for viewing: works of art excelling all but America's most exclusive restaurant fare. Fresh flowers nearly always adorned the tables. Place settings were usually surrounded on three sides with two or three rows of heavy silver plate, soup spoons sometimes as large as American serving spoons.

In Coimbra, Portugal, we knew we were eating real chicken soup when Jami dipped in her spoon and pulled out a claw.

Excepting our farewell banquet in Lisbon at the end of the guided tour when we ate beautiful filets mignon, throughout the Iberian Peninsula, where there's so much beef, we were never served a thick, juicy steak like those so common in our own country. Beef there was served in thin fried slabs, and the veal of the same shape tasted more like our beef than did the "steaks."

If you want ice-water with your meal, wait staff are happy to bring a pitcher to your table, but you'll drink it from a wine glass. Ice was available everywhere for drinks, contrary to another myth we'd heard at home, but we saw no ice machines in hotel corridors.

We wondered why we didn't see more alcoholics in Europe; wine and beer are sold in all sorts of shops: bakeries, drug stores, department stores, at exhibitions and fairs, from carts in the streets and on railroad platforms. "Bar" is an international word. One can buy bottles to-go from European bars. We drank tap water everywhere we went, even after leaving the tour, and experienced no digestive problems ourselves. (Two women in the tour group who had been drinking only bottled water were hit with cases of dysentery.)

Another report that we found to be completely untrue is that English food is dull and tasteless. Not only were all our restaurant meals varied and delicious, there were many unusual, imaginative treats in pubs, wine bars and the deli-markets. With pre-cooked foods, canned delicacies, or fresh fruits and cheeses, one can get along famously in any country without visiting a kitchen or a restaurant, and very inexpensively, depending on one's resistance to temptation.

On our first foray into a foreign food shop, we hit upon an effective international word and used it whenever we bought food or drink from locals afterward. It invariably yielded someone who spoke English.

Markets were a delight everywhere, from the tiniest village to food palaces such as Harrod's in London and the San José Market in Barcelona. Without exception, they all displayed their wares with artistry and flair, some foods looking almost plastic in their perfection. We soon learned to ask an attendant for what we wanted, having made the mistake once of literally picking out a choice ourselves, causing great distress when we

spoiled a patiently-constructed stack. With memorable irritation, the creator rearranged the pile and extracted two oranges himself for our approval.

America's condemnation of cigarette smoking did not seem to have crossed the Atlantic when we were abroad. We didn't see any smokers feel the need to apologize or to hide. Even guards in museums, where smoking is not permitted, were often spied dousing a butt when our tour group hove into view.

In Iberia, Winston and Marlboro had a virtual monopoly over other American brands. The native cigarettes weren't bad in the countries we visited, except in France where the ones we chose were too strong to smoke and almost too strong in smell to even be in the same room with (exhaust fumes are so pervasive in European cities, mere cigarette smoke is unnoticeable). In those, our smoking days, we preferred the lowest-in-tar brands, and found the equivalent everywhere. There was no government warning of a health hazard on the packages. In this and in other ways we felt freer in Europe than at home.

We often pondered the question of why some American fads, like "joggling" (as our Spanish guide called jogging) sweep across the ocean and others do not.

San Jose market on the Ramblas in Barcelona

In Paris, an old friend from the States was determined to show off to us her acquired expertise and connections with a very French meal. She took us to a tiny restaurant on a secluded street and, using her boss's name, impressed us with a dinner we may never see the likes of again. Earlier in the day, Jami and I had ducked into a café to escape snowfall after touring the Louvre and had been unable to resist a delectable lunch of Boeuf Bourguignon, herbed mushrooms and salad—much more than we ate during any other day abroad. So here we were at dinner faced with endless succulent treats and accompanying wines—and no appetite. We tried our best to stay her hand, to explain we had neither the space nor the funds to indulge ourselves or her, but she would not relent. Some of the temptations we were forced to accept:

Four goose livers with blackberries in sauce
Duck and peaches with goat cheese melted on toast
Tossed crisp lettuce salad
Plums in plum liqueur
Champagne with a floating raspberry
Belon (oysters on the half shell in some kind of
    wine sauce)
Quiche
Filet of beef with bone marrow on top
Mashed sweet potatoes
Crépes in Grand Marnier

Forgive me if I've missed ten or so items; we all chose different goodies and shared them, and Jami and I were simply too stuffed to catalog them all. You get the picture. In spite of our protests, we were forced to write a check for our entire daily budget to pay for our friend's demonstration.

Now then, examples of "dull" English fare:

—A Haworth dinner ($8.10 apiece, including a
   bottle of Mateus rosé):
Fresh trout
Venison in red wine sauce
Whole-white-onions/cauliflower/carrots/peas...
   all fresh, al dente
French fries or sliced potatoes with onion rings
Tossed salad with lettuce, onions, tomatoes,
   cucumbers, watercress
Gorgeous desserts offered, but our girth prevented
   acceptance
—A Canterbury breakfast:
Kippers
Pork and beans on fried black bread
Poached eggs with stewed tomatoes
Canadian bacon
Orange juice, coffee, wheat toast, marmalade
—A Keswick lunch in a small café on the main
street
   ($3.00 each):
John Peale pie (tender pheasant in a pastry crust
   cut into 3" x 6" wedge
Small jacket (baked) potato
Large tossed green salad with watercress and
green pepper
White wine and tea

On our own and on the tour, every meal but one was a delight. The only one that did not quite live up to our expectations was at the Casa Botín in Madrid, renowned for Hemingway's patronage. We found their specialties of roast suckling pig and roast lamb too fatty for our taste, but the restaurant is worth a visit anyway. We heard that the attractive wine pitchers that graced each table were for sale, but the restaurant had run out of the smaller ones. Upon leaving the table, Jami and I simply clutched ours to us and began to climb a corkscrew stairway with the rest of the group. Like a shot, a waiter appeared beside us excitedly indicating we'd have to pay for the pitcher. Terrific. I handed him the requested pesetas, and he squoze his way up to the desk and returned with a receipt.

Again and again, we had read or heard that all the popular American brands of cosmetics, drugs, tissues, etc. were available everywhere overseas. Once abroad, we wished we hadn't believed it. In most places, we couldn't find any suitable substitutes.

Early on, a tour guide explained the important differences between "drug stores" in Europe and America—another bit of priceless information we had not run across in our research at home. In Iberia, there were *Farmacías*, which sell curative products, both prescription drugs and patent medicine. Department stores and some markets sold toothpaste, deodorants, soap and a few cosmetics. Then there were *Perfumerías* that specialized in cosmetics and perfumes. *Drogerías*, a type of shop becoming more common, were probably what we were looking for, but we were never close enough to one to find out.

The tour brochures we'd seen hadn't mentioned that if one person in a group becomes ill, it's a good bet nearly everyone else will catch it, being cooped up together in such close quarters most of the time. I never have colds at home, so I don't know if the one I came down with on arriving in Europe was related to a first-time hemisphere change, jet lag, the soaking we got in New York, or all of the above. I soon recovered from that round.

Our tour guide could buy more effective medicine than we could, familiar as she was with the language and available remedies, and she kindly shared her cough syrup with Jami, who was barking like a seal as is her wont whenever she gets any sort of cold, and gave us the bottle to keep when we parted company. Only she didn't read us the label. After a frightening experience with the cough syrup, of which I had unwittingly taken too much, resulting in vertigo, splitting headache, and muscle spasms, we learned to ask pharmacists to read us the dosage and translate the directions.

The bug gained strength and virility as it passed through the group, and at the end of the tour, I got it back with interest. By then, it felt like pneumonia, but I didn't want it so labeled officially (which could have spoiled the trip), so we coped as best we could until we reached England, when the bug was finally defeated. Jami's version was then supplanted with a toothache. She didn't like the sound of the English dentist sobriquet "Dental Surgeon," and she knew what was wrong and what was required, being a dental assistant, so elected to wait for treatment until we returned home. Meanwhile, she muddled through, sacrificing her social image by drinking everything, hot or cold, through a straw.

We had also been informed vitamins would be easily found, but we did not find them. They are few, if sold at all. The only one we could get was vitamin C, and drugstore attendants seemed perplexed by our request. Even "natural" food stores, rare in themselves, carried few vitamins. We never found "Kleenex" per se, but there are some adequate substitutes for that. I was unable to find the kind of pressed powder I prefer, a well-known brand in America, and experimentation with other unknown quantities was expensive. The same goes for hair spray.

In Lourdes, we tried remedies locals offered us, filling up on the waters of renown, and remembering friends at home in need of healing.

Scrapbook References

For Portugal, see Pages 3-13 and 59-74

For the Montechoro Hotel, see Pages 60-61

For *Maggie Cassidy* by Kerouac on book rack in Faro, see Page 60

For Sagres, Portugal, see Page 62

For Bussaco Place in Portugal, see Pages 12-13

For Barcelona, see Pages 84-94

For Oban, Scotland, see Pages 135-136

For Edinburgh, see Pages 142-144

For York, England, see Pages 146-148

For Andalusia, see Page 32

For Lourdes (including drugstores), see Pages 77-79

THREE

On the Culture Trail
(The Eyes Have It)

THE CONSISTENT evidence of time long past left the deepest impression on us. We considered ourselves fortunate that our first contact with the deep past came on our first day on land, the 12th Century Cistercian monastery of Alcobaça in Portugal. By the second week, we had become accustomed to the enormity and complexity of ancient edifices as well as the increasingly ornate artistry, but we were glad our initial encounter was a building that presented massive simplicity and uninterrupted lines. From then on, we marveled at people going about their mundane affairs and taking for granted the wonders that surrounded them. When I'd look down and see stone steps worn concave by millions of feet through the centuries, all the various footwear these feet had worn flashed through my mind.

Churches and cathedrals in every town stunned our senses, especially when we reflected on how they'd been crafted over so many years of inspiration and faith

with only the primary tools of human hands. The priv-
ilege of actually seeing several examples of the artistry I had analyzed and drawn during years of studying
art thrilled me anew. The only disappointment—and a
big one—was the interior of Westminster Abbey. The
clutter of memorial statues we had so looked forward

to seeing were of all shapes and sizes and wedged higgledy-piggledy together, completely obscuring the architecture of the building. When we attended a service, we were sadly amused by the sermon, which stressed the difference between ego-aggrandizement and spiritual growth, the minister apparently oblivious of the stony examples all around us vying for just such ego promotion. Plastic flowers failed to redeem our disappointment.

Little machines into which one inserts a coin to learn the history of these great treasures is a modernization we became resigned to, grateful, at least, we could do even that little to ensure preservation.

Ciudad Rodrigo y Madrid

Parador palace, ancient Moorish fortress,
Roman aqueduct, table-top plateau, billboards,
*   gas stations,*
stone, oaks, cattle lands, El Corte Inglés, Galerías
*   Preciados,*
Salamanca American bar: "St. Louis Woman,"
*   "Lola," "Jezebel"*
Black olives taste like sour oil
Extensive selection of paperbacks: whole racks of
*   Agatha Christie, Erica Jong, David Copper-*
*   field*
Shakespeare and Sylvester Stallone
1,800 royal rooms
Geographical center of Iberian Peninsula

(Corte Inglés is a big chain department store, except no medicine is sold anywhere but in farmacías.

Not even aspirin or cough drops (but makeup, soap, and Kleenex—OK). Clothes upstairs: men on one floor, women and children another. Records, tapes, automotive supplies, postcards, baskets, handcrafts, junk, souvenirs—the works. The local movie theaters show last year's films, though some new to me (but not to Jami). Music on the radio largely English and American rock stars—imitators of old chestnuts, pop and classic.)

In Escorial, Hella demonstrated the acoustics in a room near the court entrance by whispering in one corner and facing a wall, and we could hear her perfectly in the opposite corner. We noted the double-headed eagle of Hapsburgs and the oldest gate in Spain with an escutcheon on it. We lunched in Toledo, viewed Hostal del Cardenal and the suckling pigs, and took pictures of El Greco and Judas trees. El Greco used only white, black, ochre, and for red, [rumor has it] the blood of pigeons. Diego Velázquez used sand from the Tagus River. The railroad station had Mudéjar architecture. La Mancha is "The Spot" with old olive trees, pointed base wine jugs, a blue fortress on a hill, and a village with one church. It also has the best cheese: queso Mancheco.

In Consuegra, the windmills were in ruins.
The Order of St. Joan of the Cross
was supposedly founded here;
Cervantes was a tax collector
and imprisoned several times.
Saffron and purple crocus
Irrigation done by donkey and wheel,

Cave dwellers and pasodobles (bull fights)
Typical dish is La Mancha Pisto served in a jug
with wooden spoons
like ratatouille.
Groves of olives
Villarta=wine press
Vente (Inn) del Quixote

The End of May might be the best time for Spain. There is always a dramatic sky with dots of window-less houses or ruins; distant villages, cities, and fields are hit by shafts of light in vast landscapes of green and red. We stayed in the only motel around and saw Gregory Peck speak Spanish on TV.

We hadn't yet investigated before going to the market a half-block up to buy gin, wine, tonic, soap, bread, and lime. They gave us a transparent plastic bag, so we stopped across the street in a shopping and shipping store (open Sunday and Monday!). I got a shopping bag woven with basket handles in dark green and white with a rooster and red and orange accents. We put the groceries in it and walked to the farmacía around the corner to buy cough medicine, Kleenex, and cream rinse, forgetting the aspirin and Listerine for which we'd gone. Later, we packed a black bag full of clothes and shipped it home, leaving only two change options. So be it.

Showers and sun alternated as we walked back at 12:30 p.m. and got into bed with gin and tonic, cheese, and figs. We were feeling poorly (head and throat, which turned into a day's pneumonia for me) but much happier on our own. Everyone was helpful and nice, and I hoped to feel up to a service and more sightseeing soon.

Marvelous monuments and empty palaces with beggars and filth made no sense. Alberto, our tour guide, said that many of the professionals—doctors and lawyers—moved away. Health note: my finger-nails are disintegrating and breaking before they reach the end of each finger—scaly, flaking, awful. Why? Never so much bread and pastry. Not enough protein and greens? Must take vitamin pills, eat eggs, fish, and meat... Jami's OK. Why me?

I'd like to walk to the top
of that furry hill to see a golden path,
five trees huddled on a crest, properly arranged.
What would be on top? Only me, expanded.

Many places are in themselves fraught with legend and renowned customs. In Portugal, we were eager to at last be able to see for ourselves the famous fishing boats of Nazaré with their painted eyes, to see them hauled up out of the water onto the beach by oxen, see the men's black long-tailed caps and the multi-petticoated women keeping warm as they waited on the beach. Alas, the eyes turned out to have been replaced by numbers, smoking tractors pulled the boats ashore, and, although it is now against the law to count the petticoats, we saw very few

women wearing any. Only one or two fishermen wore the traditional caps. At Coimbra, we expected to see students wearing capes with the edges slashed to testify to their amorous adventures. Nary a cape was to be seen.

On our way to Lisbon, we saw cork oak forests, then flat land, and then pines. Everything was sandy like in Pacific Grove and Michigan. Outside, there were fluffy clouds in the blue sky. All of Portugal was a park—any park, all parks! We went to Alcazar du Sol for port and pine candy and saw TV antennae everywhere. But, SABENA airline was such a bloody experience (never again)!

Our friend Phillipe decided to drive us "home." We stopped for cork, rock roses, and wild flowers outside of Sol. He ran out of the car and carved off a piece of cork from the forest that we kept. Setúbal was communist, industrial, busy, dirty, pretty. There was a depressive mood.

The hotel was adequate, even though it was five stars. The room was small, but everything worked. I had an awful cold, Jami a sore throat with white spots and a sore tongue. Despite that, we took off, went to Avenida da Liberdade, and walked down the boulevard to the railroad station. The façade is a great example of the intricate Manueline architectural style. Groups of men stood in the street discussing politics (I presume).

Alberto was sad about changes to his city: "Many are unemployed here, but not on welfare. U.S. money is spent on salaries for managers of the southern agricultural reform, which isn't making any money. The best schools are run by the nuns and monks who aren't allowed to live in the local communities."

Alberto showed us the Jerónimos Monastery, now empty and used only for occasional concerts. He took us to Alfama, which was a lot like Casbah: dirty with garbage and dog shit under stands of fish, live snails, vegetables and fruit. Beggars on the streets included little children, some of whom were deformed. Black Horse Square and the other monuments were unkempt.

The fado place, like the flamenco, was for tourists. Jami and I decided to go anyway and were anesthetized and happy. She got a haircut and looked adorable. We had huge oysters on shells like barnacles. The drive to Sintra was high and hilly and from Cascais to Estoril it poured rain.

We took a train ride from Lisbon and saw beautiful rich farms of eucalyptus, vineyards, fields, oaks, and cattle grazing by ruined walls. We spent the night in Pousada da Ria before driving into Aveiro; what a magnificent example of all that we love about Portugal. A nice older taxi driver took us to Tourismo and served as interpreter until we learned how to get to the inn. We drove through charming villages with new tile houses, decorated with lots of oxen with yokes. Everything was richly folkloric but passed by so quickly that no pictures were possible. At the inn, fishing occurs right outside of our window in colorful boats. Though we were damp and cold (no heat), we ate another excellent three-course dinner and went to bed at

9:00 p.m. piled high with blankets.

For breakfast, we drank big cups of coffee and took a taxi over "pavimento undulate." The bay was like glass reflecting the Phoenician boats. The sandy dunes were flat like Glen Lake. We nearly missed the train since it arrived earlier than in our schedules. The station master and ticket seller both started yelling at us and whooshed us aboard where we were able to absorb more quaint farms and vistas of the sand and pounding Atlantic.

At Oporto, we crossed a horrendous bridge and stopped. We didn't know if we should get off, but a fellow passenger took pity on us and said "Not yet." We backed across the bridge again and when the train stopped, he said, "Now." We tried to check our luggage, but there were no such lockers even though there was a sign. I drew pictures for an Information Officer who couldn't speak English. Jami and I hauled our bags and crossed a forked street twice before hailing a cab, but the driver told us that the Tourismo Office was just up the road and the ride would be too short.

As we walked uphill, our bags got heavier and heavier and I was feeling particularly rotten. We finally found the American Express, and of course, it was closed. It was only 1:00 p.m., so we sat on the step until 2:30 p.m. A nice young man then sold us train tickets straight to San Sebastián: 4 p.m. until 4 p.m. the next day! Twenty-four hours on coach and a day late. We were told to stay in Hotel Batalha that overlooked the station and is beyond description. Jami handed the address of the hotel to a woman selling strawberries and asked for directions. The woman couldn't read English, though, and thought Jami was begging and gave her a coin. We lost a few days trying to get out of Portugal along the scratched, cold, foggy coast.

Remember:

Faucets take four turns to work.
Towels harsh.
Ceramic tile in all but linoleum floors.
Emergency cord in shower.

Jami and I cleared out of our room by noon (I washed my hair), stowed our bags in the lobby, and went to the farmacía and market. We decided not to buy wine, crackers, cheese, and juice; but tea, water, and two oranges instead. I was hoping to force liquids since I couldn't shake the bug; I had taken too much cough medicine and was experiencing vertigo and muscle spasms without much sleep. My mouth was so dry it tasted of salt and my temples were splitting.

We saw little evidence of improvement resulting from the 1974 revolution in Portugal. Our sorrowful Lisbon guide bemoaned the series of six governments in five years and the exodus of many professionals to Brazil.

For tourists though, Portugal is a charming country, the people mostly warm and open-hearted, yet shy. We supposed that one or two insolent waiters we encountered may have been members of the new rebellious youth, who may be the ones who have defaced the beautiful countryside with violent graffiti slashed on seemingly every building and wall.

Nautical symbols, like the celestial globe, are incorporated profusely in Portuguese architecture.

One theory explains why there is less visual art from that country than from her neighbors: historically, men were away exploring the world rather than learning and practicing the arts. They don't lack imagination, however. An example is a tiny restaurant in a mountain village that displays a novel use for the native cork oaks.

Rossio Square

Shopping.
Buses #2, 3, and 4: five escudos.
Flowers.
All streets go to the river,
to Black Horse Square.
Tile factory, Santa Ana, taxi.

Shipping and shopping near our hotel.
Casal Mendes.
Folklore Pop Art.
Ferry boats across river.
Castle St. George missed.
Rain.
Fancy new houses, old ruins.
Didn't visit any palaces, though tried for a
    kitchen.
Too many tourists: a holiday.

A scene never to be seen at home were the crews repairing streets. In Lisbon, not only are the ornate black and white sidewalks made by hand, but so, too, are the cobblestone streets, each stone pounded in with a wooden mallet. Modern traffic whizzes by on every side.

We saw storks all over Iberia; they build their nests in the most precarious places.

SCENES ALONG THE PORTUGUESE ROAD

Why don't the men learn the secret?

Women wind down the railroad barriers;
men get the pay.

A law requires houses to be painted or whitewashed at
regular intervals. We saw only women doing so.

In spite of sharing so many common origins, the Portuguese and Spanish are very different in character. Both, however, love folklore and legends, often claiming the same one redressed as part of their own history. St. James is the favorite saint of both, and he and his cockle shells are everywhere remembered in both countries. To understand the prevalent motifs, it is imperative to know at least the legend of the rooster and the exploits of St. James.

We found the public Spaniard usually cool, proud, dignified; the Portuguese warm, humble, and shy. The Spaniard displays his Catholicism in spectacles and exterior shows; the Portuguese, more private and personal in their devotion, and they have no qualms in displaying evidences of ancient pagan beliefs in their fairytale decorations.

We were in Seville on Palm Sunday, and watched the town set up for processions of the huge floats, or *pasos*. With rain falling outside, we had to view them inside their churches, but the streets were lined with food and flower stalls and filled with milling people, both participants and otherwise. It was one of the rare occasions when young men and women could be together openly without chaperones, for which weather is no obstacle. Viewing the preparations, the incredible statues and hearing of the self-punishment the *penitentes* undergo, we maintained a reverent attitude appropriate, we assumed, to the meaning of the ceremonies.

This mood was given a rather rude jolt, however, when we saw booths on the main route of the procession openly displaying and selling girlie magazines.

Another Spanish surprise occurred when we visited the magnificent monument Franco built to the Civil War dead, the Valle de Los Cadres, a stunning basilica tunneled through a mountain top. Near this impressive sight is a small building containing restrooms and a refreshment counter.

Here loitered a group of schoolboys, none appearing older than eleven or twelve, slouching about and drinking beer, eating "Baretta" candy bars and smoking so heavily even *we* sought the icy but clean air outside.

Our tour brochure promised us a bullfight in Spain as though they didn't know (and we hadn't learned) the season began on Easter Sunday, with our tour ending on Good Friday. But we did visit one of the twenty bull rings in Malaga. We had a sturdy woman guide so burning with enthusiasm, she nearly caused us all to cast aside our former reservations about watching a bullfight. Even though unable to, we were glad to see the inside workings of a bullring.

Here, a simplified sketch of the elaborate system for safely releasing a bull, raging with frustration for having been closely confined with those wearing bells and now bent on revenge...if he's a good bull for the job, that is.

We had no idea there are so many gypsies; we saw them everywhere in Spain and soon learned to identify them by a certain cast of features, one theory being that India was the country of their origin in the far-distant past.

Once, when we were in a tiny mountain village for a rest stop, some of us were in a farm supply shop buying donkey harness bells, while outside, a gypsy woman was trying to exchange her baby granddaughter for our guide's ram's head ring. Failing to make that bargain, she asked anyone she could find for cash in payment for the baby but found no takers. (Good thing Jami was in the loo.)

We often saw gypsies at tourist attractions or in cities, selling flowers. At the Alhambra in Granada, I offered a gypsy 25 pesetas for a wilted carnation, but she demanded 50. The same woman sold Jami a fresher one in Seville four days later.

We left Madrid two days prior to elections, and none too soon. Increasingly, the streets were becoming awash with flyers, and the postered walls resembled train windows with pictures of all the same man. Every inch of space was plastered with political posters or slogans, and policemen now nestled sub-machine guns in their arms. The police are called "olives" by the citizens, because "they're green on the outside and bitter on the inside." The speed bumps to slow traffic are called "dead policemen."

It's election time and police with guns patrol the city. Every wall and lamp post is splattered with posters and on Saturday night, the streets were littered with fliers and parades. Christmas is said to be a day to be happy here: no trees, just getting drunk.

Stopped in Santa Elena, our first Andalusian village. We saw lots of straw, pottery, and jamón (air-cured ham), and continued on to La Luisiana and La Carlota, which were founded in the 18th century by a Spanish king who colonized the area; he named them for his daughters. Germans were brought in.

Our local guide said he'd decided to vote for the Socialists, because they promised such miracles for Madrid, including making it a seaport! That didn't sound all that far-fetched to us; we had already passed a project that was expending great amounts of energy and cash to change the course of a broad river. When we drove by, we saw a bridge had already been built spanning raw earth. Which reminds me of the sign on the nice new bridge at Salamanca that read "Any vehicle over [xx] tons, use the Roman bridge." So much for modern engineering.

Guarda

Cactus on table as flower
French girl in shop tries to help
a town with restaurant and public square
All the housing on stilts
Why?
Driver gives Phillipe signs
Stone walls around fields
An obelisk.

During the bus rides, Jami and I sat in front doing isometric exercises for our tension. The bus seemed to always drive in the wrong lane. Narrow streets kept us cool. There were racks of pottery by the roadside and we were told that women paint the houses white each year after it rains. We learned about Bailén ceramic style brickwork, battles between Warburton and the French, Andujar pots. Fields of limas and artichokes passed by. Eucalyptus, cypress. Gypsies originally from India. Old Moorish village with wall. Beautiful farms en route to Córdoba: cattle ranches, a few fruit trees below, and some "new" villages; white splashes in the bright green fields.

In Seneca's native land, Córdoba, a six-acre Mosque-Cathedral—the Mezquita—combines a 13th century Christian church within a mosque built in 784. It was a Muslim Mecca of the West one thousand years ago and important for olive oil, wine, cotton, leather, and silver filigree. Phoenicians had an old mill there in 700 BC. "Tower of the Bad Death" legend haunts the land.

Arrived in Córdoba proper at 12:30 p.m. Our hotel smelled only of exhaust, since there was no smog control on cars. A great staircase sucked it up from the street and into our room. Jami got the blind stuck on the window that overlooked a shaft between walls. We had time to play cribbage and though we went to bed early, we found it difficult to sleep. Too hot. We were up by the 4:30 a.m. sun and out the door by 8:00 a.m.

Spanish meals are now monotonous. I had meat I couldn't cut—like a slab of leather—and overcooked vegetables. Potatoes and desserts are always great, excepting the one apple tart that had a hair in its crust. (Ice cream good.)

Jami and I sat in front seat during an exquisite drive on an old road over mountains dotted with olive groves. We stopped for olive pickers before Baena, the village where we bought donkey bells and Amontillado sherry. I longed to see inside the white haciendas, the watch towers on top of mountains, the ruined castles, the clustered splashes of villages and miles of velvet fields. Garlic, olives, almonds. Breathtaking.

We then arrived at the foot of the Sierra Nevadas in Granada, which were spectacular. Our guide, Antonio, was kind of sloppy and conceited, but handsome. We strolled two hours through Alhambra, but dashed through the cathedral and Capilla Real where Isabel and Ferdinand are buried along with Juana la Loca, Philip the Fair, and their child, Michael. The organ inside was run by electricity. Granada was, in general, clean and cheerful. A Parador was recommended to us, but we had already spent too much on postcards, wine, and cigarettes.

A tourist mecca, our hotel in Torremolinos was gorgeous with a tile court and two big pools. We were late to a party at Julie and Sue's, so we bought wine and cheese, but weren't able to eat dinner (again). Our room was by the Mediterranean, but the beach was blocked so we couldn't go for a walk.

The next morning, we took a ferry ride to Morocco. Hotel Reina Cristina in Algeciras: miniature golf, old house, antiques, lobby, library, art show. Unfortu-

nately, we arrived after dark and left at dawn, so we couldn't enjoy it all.

Next, we drove through cattle lands in the fog. I was unable to take pictures of Gibraltar, but caught mountains, cork oaks, and little haciendas. We learned about a leader of mountain troops and the phrase, "The King had thrown an eye on her." We were in the corner of Europe, where the Mediterranean met the Atlantic.

"Big Little" lice on cacti sent to Persia to color carpets red. Lipstick has also been made from it—and Cleopatra used it—the cochinilla cactus louse. Only one family breeds it in Seville.

Caballeros and Señoritas: black hat, tight suit, leather apron, bells on skirts. Cowboys. Bull fights. Young bulls, young men: novedades. No picadors. Rejoneadores: on horseback. Torear: to fool around with bull. Only two services in Spain start on time: church and bull fights.

On the way back to our hotel, we passed pirate forts with tennis courts, and an old wall built by Arabs (rebuilt by Christians). The White Horse was punctual as the masons—who don't start on time, but end on time. Punctual as a nail.

In Jerez, we visited bodegas, or wine cellars, that aren't cellars but old monasteries with high ceilings to help even the temperature. American white oaks make for barrels that are filled with "mother" wine that is never emptied, which guarantees flavor. There are special soils for the two types of grape—palomino— that produce sherry. A "smeller" will then test it. Se-

ville had one of the richest provinces in the south with the most privately-owned ground.

In Barcelona, some of the buildings and art were left over from the International Exposition of 1929: a bust from "Marriage of Figaro," and "Barber of Seville."

Palm Sunday in Seville brought bells and archives of the Indies. There were six to eight processions and tile paintings on the walls of the Cathedral. As we walked through the alley, the temperature dropped and orange blossoms filled the air. We passed by the Maria Luisa Park, huge paintings of provinces, and the bridge over Rio Grande (Guadalquivir, or "al-wā-di al-kabīr" in Arabic), fifteen miles from the ocean. A wedding was going on in the Chapel of Macarena. We saw two floats: Pilate's judgment of Jesus and one of Mary. They were carried by 45 men; another 37 were responsible for only 10 horses.

Hairstyles: twisted braids, pearls in back, crown front. There were red roses, pearls, and gorgeous little chapels. The floats were for Good Friday. We were witness to one of the largest cathedrals in the world next to St. Peters in Rome and St. Paul's in London. Forty-seven chapels, pure Gothic. Transplendent wisteria and plum.

Lunch was delicious: gazpacho, three filets (veal, pork, beef), potatoes pan-browned, artichoke hearts, ravioli with fresh spinach and cheese sauce, and ice cream in the Hotel Luz Sevilla. After eating, it began to pour. The waiter said, "just a shower." We decided to take our chances at seeing the floats to get pictures

*and saw two beauties. Jami bought a carnation from
a gypsy for $0.30. The Cathedral was a bit gloomy,
but I got to chat about Catholicism.*

*Cemetery. Hadrian's palace. Went to Roman ruins
in the mist.*

*It rained so hard the processions were cancelled.
Thousands of chairs were strewn about the city and
roads were blocked off. We went back to the hotel, listened to classical music and ate terrific food.*

*On Monday in Manzanilla, we listened to the story
of Venus with wine while enjoying the scents of lemons
and chamomile. We boarded a new ferry on an eight-
hour trip on the way to Algarve. It's the only one that
can carry the bus, owned by a wealthy man. He was
not a very friendly man and may or may not bring the
boat back to meet us. On the way to Algarve: broad
plains, vineyards, truck farming, tile works, and little
villages pass us by. There are brilliant colors: a patch
of pink blossoms, fog, and patches of sun amidst olives
and eucalyptus. We crossed the Rio Tinto on a Roman
bridge above red water. There was a slight smell of
paper mill and rotten vegetables.*

Algarve

*Algarve is a Western city.
Not as hot as Spain with characteristic chimneys,
and towels with mirrors to ward off evil spirits
on the heads of donkeys—an Arab tradition.
People are happier, express themselves through
     dancing,
Must be the blood
only reconquered in 1249*

The '74 revolution means foreign money is now allowed.
Almond tree stories
"If they didn't die, they're still alive" legends.
Beach of three sisters
Three fountains
Three loaves of bread
Arab souls left; if you don't clear your plate, it rains

The town of Niebla was a Moorish stronghold with a huge fortified perfect wall. Heard the story about the Roman bridge in Salamanca.

Books: Ramón Sender's Carolus Rex *and H.V. Morton's* Stranger in Spain.

We had a good lunch with wine in a new parador atop a hill that overlooked the village of Ayamonte and the river Guadiana before rousing the rich yet unreliable drunk who runs the ferry. He made us wait an hour while he had his lunch. Another delay keeping us from early arrival at the hotel tonight. Rained hard on the way, clearing as we leave.

Back to Spain on our own, Jami and I hopped a cold, cold train. We could see our breath and rushed to breakfast. We went through the Pyrenees in a cold, grey fog in the land of revolutionaries.

Remember:

Maria's passport at the border
Inland farms like picture books
Chuggy train alarm heard every ten seconds
Nurseries for trees and shrubs
Fair-haired children

In Girona: tree-lined streets, old cathedral with moss-covered steps, plastic railroad station, squares with old monuments, and outdoor cafes. On these short runs, first class is a joke.

When discussing my illness and the hemisphere theory, I noticed my throat began to hurt again, and it hadn't in France. I said, "My throat hurts; I must be in Spain."

"That's a good title," Jami said, then asked, "When the moss grows on only one side of the tree, what does that mean?"

I replied, "Another good title."

We kept repeating, "Oh, Look!"

When we get off the train, nada. A tortuous walk brought us to a "vestibule" where I was able to change my francs for pesetas. We ate soup, salad, and tea before heading into the Info Office. Due to a convention in town, all of the hotels are full. We were told where to go for a ferry but it was suggested that we return after siesta.

We checked our bags in lockers and walked (and walked) to Ramblas. Then we walked some more to the Oriente Hotel: full. We tried a hotel agency and were told, "Not one room in all of Barcelona." There were hundreds of hostels and pensiones everywhere, but we were too squeamish; we avoided a specific one because all of the men in the lobby were unfriendly. We tried another, The Royal. "Yes," the concierge said, "It costs 3,000 pesetas." Our limit was two, but I said, "We'll take it," because we still had to collect our bags. I was made to pay in advance—$60 per night!

When we were let into our room after a trip to the Picasso Museum, we realized it was one they saved for suckers. It had a filthy rug and a view of the hole. Oh well, better than the park, though the price rankled. Only one night. In search of food, we spotted a Wimpy's. How good a hamburger sounded, but we were given old buns, no mayo, and for the first time, poor French fries. With beer, it came to $8.50. Barcelona is the most expensive place we've found. Disappointed but full and undaunted, we returned to The Royal for bed by way of Ramblas with a stop at the fabulous San José market where we bought enormous pears and took pictures.

I looked again in the book stands for Cuentos de la Alhambra by Washington Irving to no avail.

The next morning, we had to make a big decision about whether or not to take a ferry that day or stay in Barcelona. We decided that if we found a room, we'd stay. We meant to check out Gaudi Hotel, but walked across the street to "Residio" and got a room for 2,000 pesetas no problem. Jolly English-speaking concierge in an old grand residence room with French windows and a balcony overlooking Ramblas. In our room were carved wooden bedsteads, chairs painted in red and silver, and a big maple in new leaf in view. We were so happy.

Next to the hotel was a travel agency where we booked ferry tickets and changed money. We walked to the Maritime Museum, which had fabulous medieval shipyards where Columbus' ship was built. There was a wonderful display as well as a full-scale replica—or possibly real—ship with oars from the 15th century. We studied it until the museum closed at 1:30 p.m. Next, we walked to the Costume Museum thinking it would be open late—wrong. We hunted food and found Amaya, a recommended Basque restaurant. Clean and cozy, we had soup, French fries, and lamb; the latter was more like veal fried in batter.

The jolly maître d' gave us an elevated table in back to see the touring dance troupe that was set to perform. I analyzed all the dancers and the star this time was fiery and vulgar, but still great. We stayed five-and-a-half hours and went down to the bar after the show to congratulate our favorite. I got the autograph of one male dancer and was sorry I passed by the other; we didn't like his schmaltz, but he was good. We walked home at 2:30 in the morning.

The Costume Museum was next to the Picasso Museum and housed clothing from the 15th to 19th centuries in an old palace building dating to the 1400s. We wanted to see earlier items but realized they would be too hard to find. After a cab ride to Montserrat mountains, we went to Pueblo Español hoping to buy a shawl and a comb. I did buy a dress for Anne M., but no luck on flamenco shawls. I got a chip for John Gourley from a tile store that was being restored (or renewed). I began to feel woozy.

We grabbed paella for lunch and, during a rain shower, hailed a cab to Gaudi Park. I was feeling nauseated and chilled. We looked for a restroom, but the Museo was closed. It took ages to get back to our hotel, where I collapsed for two or three hours.

When I awoke the next morning, I felt a bit better, so we dressed and walked to the Opera House Liceo. Such fun! The day before, I babbled at a lady at what I thought was the ticket window while Jami hunted "seating" in the dictionary. The lady finally got through to me we were at the wrong window. We found the right one with a "mapa" of the theater and picked our seats. The theater had the best acoustics of any opera house in the world. Fascinating old boxed seats faced backwards. Even though I had to go straight to the bar to get water upon arriving at the opera, I enjoyed the performance and we walked home at midnight.

We re-packed in the morning, dressed, had breakfast, and caught a cab to the wharf where we waited over an hour to board. We were disappointed when we got inside the cabin, but at least it was a cabin. We ate more paella in the café and sat in squishy seats at the prow overlooking the Riviera.

Iberians say "Jesús" when you sneeze.

End of Spain.

Adiós.

IN SWITZERLAND, *Greige patchwork fields filled the mountain sides. Fuzzy trees of forest green and leather-like mauve rivulets against the rock; finger thrusts of snow reached down on the peaks amid a row of fluffy orange and chartreuse. Hang gliders looked like kites or birds. Heidi houses were high on the meadows. Red and yellow tulips hung against grey walls. How to get there? The village was completely surrounded by vineyards.*

Montreux on lake—wow! Snow in crevices.

We met a black woman singer who worked as a model but didn't like it. An older Swiss gentleman came on strong and bugged her, asking her if she wanted to see his flat in Lausanne. A young American photographer who "mostly does beauty" shots also talked to her. I was self-important: I love, I think, I feel. Touch, touch. Many friends in many ports. Mundane philosophy.

"It's always nice when you take a train and meet somebody you like, 'cause you don't always."

"Yes, it's nice to meet someone who can speak..."

In Scotland, names for the Aviemore Clan Tartan Center: Scott, Roe, Sherwood, Robinson, Smith, Elliott, Flaherty, Strowbridge, Carmichael, Nelson, Gourley, Whitaker. [Ed. Note: Family lore indicates that Sir Walter Scott is Carolyn's sixth great uncle. She and Jami were excited to visit his home in Scotland, Abbotsford House.]

Birds: fully musical sounds in all of England and Scotland. Rooks or ravens?

I rode in the back of the train with a good-looking gent (Leslie Howard type with strong features). He was well-dressed and on his way home from a business trip, checking stock in various west coast cities. He caught a river trout a few days ago and was looking forward to it for dinner, though that wouldn't be until 9 p.m. We talked of accents and he said Inverness folk spoke perfect English without an "English" accent. We later learned Dubliners do, too. Boys from a football game got on and we loved how we couldn't understand a word they said. Should we have tried to speak their language, as we did in Spain?

Jami and I arrived at the bus station at 9:10 p.m. and an inspector told us where we could find a private hotel. We walked a block and a half by whole rows of old, clean houses. We went into the Windsor Hotel and got a back room overlooking horses, stone houses, and the sea. We went out for beer and brought back two cans of bitters, had our cob [bread] and cheese sandwiches in the room, and read.

We thought we'd miss the 10:00 a.m. bus, but even though we started breakfast at 9:15, we were at the bus station by 9:50. We arrived in Glasgow at 11:45 with the next bus set for 4:15 p.m. The station was surrounded by rubble in a crummy part of town; no greenery. I ran out of hair spray and looked a sight; Jami's teeth ached. Here the sky was a brilliant blue and sunny, but there were no picnics and nothing scheduled on Sunday, not even a movie. We walked up a dead street that was being made into a mall, but no shops—or liquor stores—were open yet.

We finally found a bar and shared a pint and fish and chips and ate in the middle of the street before heading back to the bus station for coffee. This was our first negative experience: Jami in pain, me unhappy. What a shame. But there was no sign of "Scotland" other than posters and the burr. The bus had big band 40s music like "I'm Beginning to See the Light" and other pleasant songs. Strange drinks were made, and we wanted to learn what they were. We used our bus pass to Inverness for the last time. We should have seen more of Ayr.

Glasgow was full of old ornate buildings covered with black and fronted by plastic shops or warehouses with garages below. We passed a book-maker and a large old building housing both the museum and an art gallery near the cathedral. Lots of litter and posters on the ground—trying to improve. Down the river, Clyde and Firth were lined with huge two- and three-story homes, and colorful sail boats docked on both sides. We stopped into the Green Kettle Tea Room for tea and scones as the grey sky lowered ahead.

On the drive back, we took a long, five-minute break at Loch Lomond. We tried to follow the map, but no towns were listed. It was a fun, roundabout trip. The lake ends by green pastures of sheep, sheer moors, rushing creeks, woods, waterfalls, and rocky land. It must be heavenly in the summer and a fisherman's paradise. The snow on the peaks was the best yet on our way to Oban. The trees were bare, and the people were handsome, a winter landscape.

The beautiful entrance to Oban was on the water, a lovely little fishing harbor. Sheep grazed the water's edge and the bus stopped in front of Caledonian Hotel. We walked in bedraggled. The girl at the desk said, "All booked up," but a handsome older gent with a pint informed us that the guest house around back had room. We walked to an ornate stone building. It had only one double bed left for $6.50 (including breakfast). It was a big room with a window over the bay. On the way, we saw an ad for Highland Piper and dancing that night, which wouldn't have known if we'd stayed in *the Caledonian!*

There were three baths in a row near our room in the hallway. We tried to do something with our hair and at 9:30 p.m. went to McIntosh's Kitchen to listen to black folk singers for half an hour. Then, a big retired chief piper of The Glasgow Pipe Band and a bemedaled 12-year-old lassie marched in and played on their bandstand. An accordion player followed, but at least played cultural music. The hotel was crowded, but we went back for lovely bed and awoke to rain and fog.

We drove north along what must be waterways. I felt so good, so at home, and took pictures of a castle on Loch Ness. We caught the train from Inverness to Aviemore and Pitlochry before our passes expired at midnight. Inverness is a small village, but a theme-park-like energy is emerging with ski lessons, riding, skating, climbing, Santa Claus barrel racing, and bumper cars. The center, too, has mostly tartans in ties, but with few kilts, cloth, or mufflers. We got on the computer to input our data on Scott, Robinson, Elliott, and Carmichael. Before boarding the train, we stopped in a bar for a pint for me and a gin for Jami's teeth.

On the train to Pitlochry, we ate beef burgers (buns better than ours) and drank rosé. We also bought extra bottles hoping to have a perfect day in Pitlochry. My heart was in the highlands. Snow was on the hills, but the air was fresh and balmy. The rocky hills were barren, but the heather will probably bloom in the summer. The oceanside idyllic scenes of streams, pastures, and trees had a few farm houses. When we arrived in Pitlochry at 7:00 that evening, we were beside a beautiful gated garden and "Fisher's Hotel." We went in through the back door and took a room, tearing up to number 33 to get our boots on.

We noted a play at 8:00 p.m. and after walking the wrong way and then asking for help, we made it, sitting in the second row. It turned out to be "Private Lives" by Noel Coward. Darling theater full of all kinds of people.

We managed to get to a chemist's for life-saving hairspray (though still too weak) and medicine for Jami's teeth (ditto) before catching a train back on Saturday. A scruffy chef sat next to Jami and gulped from a pint of Scotch, apologizing that he'd been to a pub this late and his "head is a bit fuzzy." It was chilly out; the sun was up but the sky threatened clouds.

We had high hopes for sun in Edinburgh, but had to change at Perth because of a damaged tunnel. We sat across from a gorgeous sandy-haired, big-eyed youth who noted the young stag we saw leap over a pasture fence. He blushed when I said, "I hope they don't shoot them here." "I hope not, too," he said. He'd been to Florida for a month.

We took a stuffy carriage to Edinburgh, but found the largest, most efficient Info Center. Unfortunately, they booked us into an attic of a private hotel at the bottom of a steep hill with circular stairs. We strolled down to Grassmarket for gifts and up the steps to Royal Mile, but read that Holyrood House was closed. We discovered a great restaurant for dinner. A lonely single man sat opposite, but...

Walking home, we decided that one's impressions

of a city depend a lot on one's accommodations. A feeling of expansion and beauty? Cramped and dull? Be careful of judgments. I was thinking of how I felt bummed at the beginning and could then look out over cluttered buildings and our garret with its sloping side windows. I looked at the rows of wild clouds, street lights and felt like I was in a scene from Dickens. I'm living in Edinburgh. My garret is like dozens of others. I'm a part of it, not a tourist.

An old woman alone, unafraid, and the constable shy. The yellow gaslights, the sloping roofs, the night-life below. The castle at the end of the row, an old kirk near the block's end. Thank God for allowing me to see this!

Scheduled entertainment on the tour generally disappointed when it was billed as a sampling of true ethnic culture, or típico. In Tangier, although the Moorish banquet hall was exquisite and the feast delectable, and some of the entertainers talented, we were disgusted by the eventual decline of the show into tasteless Las-Vegas-like stunts, such as when a buxom belly-dancer undressed a middle-aged patron after shaking her ample bosom in the face of an elderly man.

In a típico Lisbon restaurant, an exhibition of Fado and folk dances ended with a similar performance, so we skipped one of the planned entertainments at our Algarve hotel. Did we go to the old countries to be disillusioned?

Independent in Barcelona we hunted down some less popular flamenco (a word we hadn't known means "Flemish," though no one seemed to know why). A

club named Los Tarantos was recommended, but we went there for an additional reason. Years before, we had been enamored with a movie by that name filmed near Barcelona and featuring the Carmen Amaya dance troupe, a famous company of gypsy flamenco dancers. We had dinner at the Amaya Restaurant and proceeded to the club. We had never been able to find a translation of the name, so when the host showed us to a table we asked him, here at the horse's mouth. His reply: "It doesn't mean anything in English; it's the name of a movie."

We had just ordered wine when a tour group filed in and our high expectations briefly plummeted. Although the club was part of somebody's tour, the dancing did turn out to be better than what we'd seen on ours, even though some of the girls looked more like American models than gypsies. After the show, we followed the tourists out, but were stopped by the host.

"You're not leaving? The best is yet to come."

We scurried back to our table and felt very "in" as only a few avid fans surrounded the stage. For this show, the girls had changed their costumes, more men dancers appeared, and the star of the club made her appearance. She was all we had hoped for: Maruja Garrido, a gypsy woman no longer young, but wild, abandoned, expert and fiery like Carmen Amaya. Finally, after five and a half straight hours, our appetite for flamenco was appeased.

A block or two from our hotel in Barcelona was the world-renowned Gran Teatre del Liceu opera house, the greatest in the world when it opened in 1857 and still considered second best for acoustics. We wanted to see something there, and it so happened the Tokyo Ballet was to perform. Avid dance enthusiasts, we were pleased.

In the afternoon, we went to the box office to get our tickets, marching up to the nearest window. The lady behind the bars did not speak English, but on the wall was a placard listing the various seat prices. I spelled them all out to Jami who consulted the dictionary. After ten to fifteen minutes of this, during which the lady was vainly trying to tell us something, we needed to find out where the seats were located.

"What we need is a diagram of the seating," I declared, "look up 'diagram.'"

Jami did so.

"Mapa," was the simple answer. Triumphantly, I turned back to the lady in the cage.

"Dónde esta un mapa?"

Having patiently waited for us to conclude our charade, her pointing finger now got through to us. Opposite her window in the lobby was another, and there, sure enough, was a diagram of the seating just like those at home. The tickets cost more than we'd ever paid even for box seats, and the performance didn't begin until 10:30 p.m. A siesta is a necessity if you plan on attending the theater in Spain.

How long we had dreamed of seeing the Prado and the Louvre! And now, at last, we were actually going to walk their hallowed halls and feast our eyes on countless "originals." Well, we saw the buildings, all right, but not much of the contents. I suppose guidebooks

aren't likely to discuss the fact that unless the sun is shining brightly outside, which it rarely is, many of the rooms are so dark, the paintings are all but invisible. The thrill of seeing Goya's "Dos de Mayo" and "Tres de Mayo" was considerably dimmed. The guide looked embarrassed but told us a wing was being built to remedy the situation.

One should also expect that in every gallery one or

another room or wing is going to be closed for some reason or other—particularly the one you especially wanted to visit. And, as for the original Mona Lisa, she is so small and protected, all you can see is your own reflection in her glass, if you can get close enough to see even that. Be forewarned, as well, that many of the buildings you've come so far to see will be covered with scaffolding, as the eternal chore of cleaning and repairing goes on. All this we could accept, but it would have been nice to know about ahead of time.

A discovery of a happier sort was the amazing number of clocks displayed in all the palaces and museums, as well as one or many in every town no matter how small—and every one ticking away in perfect time, no matter how old. We wondered about this in contrast to our own country. In our town, if there's a visible clock at all, it is often wrong or broken, even in airports. Yet we are passionate about time-keeping.

Since to us London itself is one vast museum and gallery, we were delighted to discover the programs of walking tours to scout out specific attractions. Of course, we signed up for a "Dickens Walk" and were led through parts of the city that revealed many of his sources, which would have gone totally unnoticed had

we not had a guide. Even our guide appeared to be a character from the master's pen. Every now and again he would stop to read poetry to us or other relevant literary tidbits, invariably perched unwaveringly on his tiptoes. We packed our bags on High Street, then walked the town tour, which included several places Dickens used in his stories and Oh Joy, the Chalet was in the garden of the old museum; one of his houses, too. The Cathedral was loved and cared for with beautiful floors and a yellow sepia design. We visited the

Chapter House and didn't even have to cover our shoes. The Crypt was eerie, though. We came across a few names in the graveyard that inspired Dickens: they're almost obscured now, but I saw a "Dorrit." We also passed the castle and the River Medway he knew as a child and ate at the Bull Hotel, or the "Blue Boar" in Great Expectations.

In our search for the Brontë background, nothing could deter me from trodding the heather-topped moors in search of *Wuthering Heights*, or the supposed prototype for it, Top Withens. After reading the straightforward booklet, "How to Keep From Dying on the Moors," we set out in a slashing, icy rain through and around horses, lambs, long-haired sheep, mud and spongey heather on the four-mile trek from Haworth. Midway, we stopped to huddle on a bench against a stone wall to eat our packed lunch of hot tea, "nutty whole meal cob" bread, cheese, apples and watercress sprouts. Our mouths were full of rain as well, and we howled with laughter at each other's drowned-rat appearance. In the end, it was Jami who hollered "uncle" and persuaded me to turn back before our quest was completed. Not to be entirely daunted, I took a snapshot of an abandoned farm that looked to me equally as likely to have been Emily's model for *Wuthering Heights*.

In Haworth, England, on the trail of the Brontës, we hopped on the local 665 bus. Bradford station was a surprise: big and organized with lower level concourse escalators. But the conductor spoke little English and since we couldn't understand—or vice versa—we got off at the Info Center and walked back to town. It was still open and the clerk called the Black Bull Inn and booked us one of the five bedrooms. She called the town's one taxi and we were swept up onto the cobbled street as it rained.

We rang the doorbell there and, in time, Mr. Bennett came down and let us in, helping us to the back door and into our room at the head of the stairs, unsmiling and terse. He was a handsome man in his early 40s, who scooted his stockinged feet across the hall to his own quarters. The bathroom (shared by all, family too) and the stairs separated us. We noted the bar was well stocked and the artificial gas fire was going; there was also an enormous German shepherd dog. It henceforth occupied the landing during the day.

We opened our door to a pale-pink-flower wallpapered room that slanted downward toward the steep street below. It had two wooden beds, one higher than the other emphasizing the slant; the dresser so low, its mirror only showed you from feet to waist; a big TV; another false fireplace that ate ten pounds [sterling];

a recessed window with red, white, and grey flowered curtains; a mantel piece; an awful painting hung opposite a too-small glass ship; a sink with two pink and white hand towels; one large orange bath towel on a hook; and a mirror too high to see anything but the top of your head. Large lavender and navy flowers with green leaves sit atop a wood-veneered wardrobe. Beige carpet. The white chenille bedspreads were a relief, though lots of heavy blankets forewarned us. All of its oddities added to our fun, and nowhere did we have better food than in the dining room.

In the pub below our room, Branwell Brontë, the troubled alcoholic brother of Charlotte, Emily, and Anne, had hastened his demise. *It was deserted all afternoon and we wondered at its non-attendance, except for the dog. We put more sweaters on and went outside to explore surroundings. All the shops were closed except one book store where we bought Charlotte Brontë's early works and Daphne de Maurier's* The Infernal World of Branwell Brontë. *The Brontë museum at the Parsonage was very well done. There was little of Emily, but we noted her view from the window in her tiny room. A hodgepodge of green-mossed and grey tombstones lay between her, the rugged church, and the walled-in fields beyond.*

Back at the hotel, we asked a lad if they served dinner. He said, "Yes, at 7:00," so at that hour we descended the stairs to see the bar filling with people. We were drinking gin and tonics when a darling little round grey-haired lady gave us the dinner menu with her broken wrist. We ordered venison, guinea fowl, three fresh veggies, two potatoes, a huge salad with water-cress sprouts, and a bottle of Mateus Rosé—wow!

After dinner at the pub that night, we had scotch and pints and talked to three Yorkshire lads. One was a lorry driver, one into furniture, and one was a WWII vet. They had to leave at 10:30; only residents can continue drinking at night. They were resigned to it and told us funny stories about drunk driving laws. We went to bed early after deciding to stay another night.

26,400 + 10,000 + 9,400 + 18,600 + 123,000 = 187,400

$230 train transfer to Paris

We were "knocked up" for breakfast at 9:00: eggs, fried bread, bacon, sausage, and tomato for me, while Jami had pork and beans on toast with an egg! Toast with Dundee [marmalade], of course, and coffee. We returned to the Info Center for future bus schedules, bought a book about the Brontës and while Kathy [the clerk] wrapped it for us, she told us about her family in Haworth. When I asked if she was interested in [the Brontës], she said, "The Brontës weren't the only family with tragedies."

Still, "My great-grandfather was the town barber and cut their hair" was a fact that gave her pride. She had the physiognomy of a rag doll: a boneless face, soft and settling into chin, and tight sleeves that appeared stuffed. We wondered if the Brontë girls might have been similarly built. Then, next door at the post office, the terse postmaster had me undo some of Kathy's tape and replace it with a few pieces of string *so I could send it book rate. I filled in all the forms, stuck on stamps, and tossed it into the bag. Cost: £1.18 We also bought three sheep skins that we spotted on our walk up the hill (lamb) for £7 ($14) each, plus £1.50 ($3) for shipping. £26 total.*

For lunch, we ordered a "nutty whole meal cob," cheese, milk, fruit, mayo, and watercress sprouts before setting off for the moors. The sun had earlier threatened a time or two, but the day rapidly became misty and rainy. We took pictures in the graveyard, in pastures with horses and on a path full of puddles and slippery black earth. The brisk wind howled as we reached the moors. When we stepped away from the shelter of the stone wall, I could lean against it. Everywhere sheep and lambs. We stopped on a sheltered bench and ate our delicious repast, or part of it, saving the milk and fruit. Our wet hair whipped about our heads. Our shoes were wet, but not cold. Our "thin skins" kept us warm. But Oh, my ears!

We passed an abandoned farm house that looked like my idea of Top Withens, the inspiration for the house in Wuthering Heights, *and got as far as the falls. Ahead of us stretched endless sodden and windy moors. We decided the pictures of my Top Withens were enough and I was of the opinion that even frail Emily would not have walked that far, when there were so many other similar houses nearer. So, we turned back and climbed over the brown about-to-bloom heather amongst the long-haired sheep and lambs. The wind behind us made our return easy, though our shoes were wet and stained with black mud.*

On our way back to the hotel, we changed buses at Keighley and I read a new magazine with the best article yet. In the room, Jami bathed as I set my hair before going downstairs for another great meal: a beef steak, a ham steak with pineapple, a pork steak with whole mushrooms, a big piece of liver, a fried egg, lettuce, tomatoes and cucumbers, and sausage. On the side: fresh whole baby carrots, zucchini, and round fried potatoes—whew! Jami had pork in marsala and cream. White wine. After eating, we went into the pub and ordered the cider the three young men had told us about. A man tried to engage Jami in conversation, but we sat apart from him; we were so tired and warm and sleepy.

The next morning, we ate breakfast at 8:00 and walked down to Changegate. A nice lady helped us find the bus. It was lovely country: more rock fences snaking up green pastures full of sheep, stately stone houses, stone villages, stone bridges, and more trees. The air was thick with fog for part of the journey. However, Kendal was large and getting touristy, as was Windermere.

In the rain, the lake looked like a slab of polished slate, with ridges. We saw more pines, woods, and fields of peach-colored heather. But I'm not too impressed with Keswick; it is large and busy, more so than what we've seen elsewhere. A man at the bus station was rude and unhelpful. We had lunch of "John Peale Pie" (pheasant), two small baked (jacket) potatoes, a large green salad with lots of green peppers, and wine, all for £1.50.

*We walked all over trying to find the Info Station,
but signs led us around in a circle. We resigned to take
the local bus to Carlisle and needed a bank, but none
were open. Using our heads, we read the info book and
saw that there were different kinds of information stations: national, regional, and local. Oh. We were sent
to a Scottish bus line station and an inspector told us
all we needed to know: the bus for Ayr was in front of
us, but full, so we were escorted onto another while the
other bus would wait for us at the next stop. There was
a hamster on the bus due to an incident in Carlisle.*

In Scotland, the big surprise was that the burr is still
so strong; most Scots might as well be speaking Greek
for all we could understand—and they really did say
"wee" for something small. I don't know if we expected
most men to be going about in kilts, but we certainly expected to see some. As it was, the only traditional
dress we saw was in floor shows or at Edinburgh Castle.

In all of Britain, there seems to be no known for-
mula to guide your pronunciation of names. Maybe it's
their way of getting even with us rebellious colonists.
For instance, one must go to Keighley to get a bus for
Haworth. We avoided pronouncing the name until after
we'd heard a native speak of it, and she said, "Keithley."
Who would ever suspect the "g" would be changed to
a "t"? But on the Pitlochry train platform, we were
ashamed of fellow-countrymen (or their education)
loudly discussing "Eden Burg." Later we learned any
name with an "est" or a "w" in the middle; skip it.

On bus rides through Britain we enjoyed signs
along the way and tried to translate some into an Amer-

ican equivalent. Divided highways there are "dual carriageways," a cul-de-sac is a "close," parking lots ask, "Have you payed and displayed?" That one startled us a bit at first sight, as did a sign beside the road next to a horse farm: "No studs or lines for miles." For several hours, we thought it referred to horses. Instead of exits, they show the "way out," a slang expression still in vogue at home, but meaning something else. For miles and miles, we'd see signs advising the motorist to "Take Courage," and we thought perhaps it was a leftover admonition of Winston Churchill's, or something. But when in the pub at the Black Bull, a lorry (truck) driver explained to us that it was the name of a beer and also that "This is a free house" meant the pub was not franchised by any brand of spirits, such as Courage beer. At first sight, that sign raised some questions and our eyebrows.

Well, just as we marveled at the ignorance of the "Eden Burg" couple, so many a reader is doubtless marveling at our own educational gaps and blocks. A better course is to go marvel at other parts of the world and at the impossibility of ever seeing or knowing it all.

Scrapbook References

For Alcobaça in Portugal, see Page 6

For Portuguese churches and cathedrals, see Pages 6-7

For Rodrigo and Madrid in Spain, see Pages 24-27

For Escorial in Spain, see Page 23

For Toledo in Spain, see Pages 28-30

For La Mancha, see Page 31

For Coimbra, see Pages 9-11

For Setúbal, see Page 64

For Alfama, see Pages 65-66

For the drives to Sentra and to Estoril, see Page 67

For the train ride to Lisbon, see Page 76 (map)

For Oporto, see Pages 72-74

For Hotel Batalha, see Page 74

For native cork oaks as art, see Page 14

For the storks of Iberia, see Pages 4 and 16

For the Portuguese legend of the rooster, see Page 3

For the exploits of Saint James, see Page 18

For Portuguese architecture, see Pages 9-10

For Seville, see Pages 53-58

For Malaga and bullfights, see Pages 40-44

For inner workings of bullrings, see Page 43

For the Alhambra in Granada, see Pages 38-39

For Madrid, see Pages 24-27; see map Page 24

For Andalusian village, see Page 32

For Salamanca, see Pages 15-18

147

EPILOGUE

Over and Above

HEREIN WE HAVE shared only a few samples of our travel surprises in the hopes of being helpful and increasing your pleasure abroad. In even so limited a visit, we learned a great deal every day, and our perspective toward our own country and our own lives was markedly changed. One lesson stands out in our memories, one we hope to retain henceforth:

En route, in our efforts to "be prepared," we wasted much valuable energy trying to anticipate what might lie ahead. "What if...?" was our continuous concern. Well, of course, there's no way we could guess at conditions so unfamiliar, and invariably what occurred were situations we could not have foreseen. It took a lot of practice and constant reminding of each other to keep the point of view our tour guide expressed when we anxiously asked her, "what if...?" She replied, "when it happens, we'll deal with it then." This is by far the best attitude to assume once all known steps have been taken.

On our return flight, this lesson was tested. Our plane was struck by lightning, and when the Captain none-too-reassuringly called all personnel to their emergency stations, we merely reached for each other's hands and calmly waited for "it" to happen, grateful we'd been allowed the trip at least once in our lives. Obviously, "it" was not quite THE END.

BON VOYAGE!

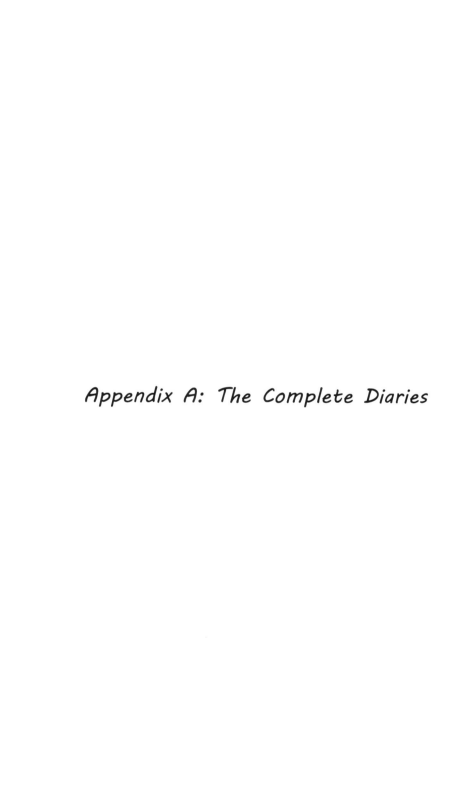

Appendix A: The Complete Diaries

ENGLAND

No ONE (BANK or change place) would cash my £ travelers' checks. Nevertheless, I signed three and we boarded the train to Boulogne. Across from me and Jami was a typical British bloke: coordinated checkered tweeds reading *Memories of a Fox-Hunting Man*. Welcome to England! On the phone last evening, Mr. Haggis said, "Welcome Home."

May 3rd, 1979

Language problem: so used to thinking Now, how do I say that? when on this train. Jami wanted to buy lunch from the cart and turned to me saying, "How do you say, 'How much?'" and, previously thinking of a question for Mr. Haggis, I began to translate. An English couple had French bread and cheese, cookies, and apples (no liquid); we had wine and sandwiches.

On the way to Rochester, we had the back seat to ourselves. I imagined Dickens riding this road, seeing the old houses and gardens—everywhere in bloom! Signs read: "Tobaccos, Wines & Fancy Goods" and "Dual Carriageway." The Tourist Office was open when we arrived, but nothing else.

We packed our bags on High Street, then walked the town tour, which included several places Dickens used in his stories and Oh Joy, the Chalet was in the garden of the old museum; one of his houses, too. The Cathedral was loved and cared for with beautiful floors and a yellow sepia design. We visited the Chapter House and didn't even have to cover our shoes. The Crypt was eerie, though. We came across a few names in the grave-yard that inspired Dickens: they're almost obscured now, but I saw a "Dorrit." We also passed the castle and the River Medway he knew as a child and ate at the Bull Hotel, or the "Blue Boar" in Great Expectations.

On to Faversham

Everything was closed up tight, though people were in the streets. We saw a block of buildings in mid-street and a central well with pink paint and the Tudor rose on it. Charming town.

Then on to Canterbury by back roads—lovely farms. We got there at 5:00, but it had taken all day to drive 50 miles. We arranged for a bus to Rye the next day and walked down its main street of old Elizabe-than buildings and Roman remains (exhausted), and passed through a great wall to a gate that the bus had to squeeze through. The tourist office was closed, but we turned back just as a man was leaving, so he went back in to call some hotels for us: no baths.

Finally, we stayed at the County Hotel, four stars and a nice downstairs room, bath, and color TV. But it had a tacky color and thin towels with cheap bedding (Woolworth's) but Oh Joy, we washed in the tub just before the radiator cooled. We went out for groceries but all had already closed, so I had a horrible sandwich. There was no service in the coffee shop or in the hotel.

But then delicious bath, Harvey Cream and ten hours of sleep and rarin' to go in the morning. We saw a cathedral, shopped, packed, and got the bus at 12:10 p.m. Beautiful countryside surrounded wealthy old manor houses and picture-book farms.

In Ashford, the bus station girl said, "You're lucky. The bus to Rye only runs on Tuesday at 2:10 p.m.," and it was only 1:00 p.m.! It was a clean, large town with a brand-new-looking Norman church, but Jami complained of no entertainment.

We had a lunch of steak and mushroom pie with chips (great French fries) for only £3.24. No salads, "too expensive." We caught the crowded bus to Rye; I'd have missed it if Jami hadn't been watching the other way. There was a survey for bus service on board and when I began writing comments, a lady behind me said, "Hun, you don't have to write a ten-page article, you know," but in a very jolly tone. Everyone in England is friendly and sweet.

Canterbury Cathedral was surrounded with fresh flowers and the same atmosphere of love and care as Rochester. Repair work in progress: dreadful destruction, an exhibit being built in the crypt—to think it survived the bombs—and new stained-glass windows with Disney-like faces that were too garish. Other windows were exquisite.

East Sussex

We took the long way 'round to Rye, which was full of brick houses, sheep, lambs, cattle, fabulous country homes, and ever-blooming tended gardens. The fruit orchards in Kent were all in bloom, too. Next was Appledore, a neat, beautiful little village with sheep, geese, and immaculate hedges. Sunny day, warm with a cool breeze, fields of flowers and a creek with fish.

There were country lanes with Norman or Saxon churches, and the railroad gates were opened and closed by hand. But Rumer [a friend] no longer lives in Lamb House and unfortunately for us too, it isn't open on Tuesdays, so we boarded a different bus to Eastborne and then to Brighton.

I'm learning we have not been inquiring about "coaches," the express service. I happened to see a bus change its sign and so we got on half an hour early, but it then turned around and faced the other way. We'd never have even seen it had I not *happened* to look at that moment. So, then we weren't meant to see this ancient and fascinating town. Others await.

We took a double-decker bus to Icklesham and saw an incredible farm house with a brick cottage with a garden, dog, and sheep at the gate. I think the windmills signal a Dutch influence and it was the most beautiful yet with country homes right out of a movie. We glanced a bus-load of schoolchildren from Rye to Hastings, the bay, a watch tower, and briefly saw a huge Norman castle in the glen.

Hastings had rows of uniform brick houses on one side of the hill that were painted on their back sides; "public conveniences" that were crowded; old intermingled churches; pot-bellied Tudor shops; a fort overlooking the bay; and a touristy waterfront. It was a bit grimy on first view without the charm of Rye, but we didn't have time to explore. Still, there was a clean rock beach for a big city. Sign: "Have you paid and displayed" in the parking lot.

Scaffolds are everywhere and the bus stops at every other pole. There was a pleasure palace built out over the water and we saw shops, restaurants, dancing, white-washed domes, and little towers. There were rows of houses facing long meadows with steps to the sea and other bunches of houses on the beach. Are they watchtowers in those back yards or storage tanks? Converted? The seaside country, clean roadsides, and well-kept farms are beyond belief.

Brighton

The bus stopped and waited to let a child use the toilet on the side of the road, so we arrived at six when everything had already closed. We were given coach times for tomorrow, since there were no more for today. (We asked if we could get any farther tonight and he suggested taking a bus to Worthing.) We did see the Royal Pavilion: not as expected. It's a faint dot on the map, so we prepared ourselves by observing houses along the waterfront as we moved along in the sunset.

We were sure Worthing would be asleep by the time we got there. We also had to pay. A young conductor explained that only some bus lines were covered by our passes and showed us which ones in our brochures. Well, it was only £_____. He was very helpful in pointing out closed coach offices and, much to our delight, a lovely square nearby surrounded by hotels. Of course, we aimed for the three-star (highest) and got another luxury room and bath for £22 (or that many dollars)—sigh. We had sandwiches and wine in our room, but yet another toilet had to be pumped and the "hot" and "cold" water faucets in both the sink and the shower did not work.

The next morning, we were early to the station after kippers, sausage, and poached eggs for breakfast (included in room rate). A nice lady gave us contrary information to the man in Brighton: the coach was so slow, but we had to take it and pay £2 for the bus! We sat by the sea and watched fishermen clean fish in front of customers who came along to buy right out of the boat *Danny Boy*. Next, we passed Arundel, but the castle was too remote to even photograph—too bad. Then we passed Holiday Park, which had a great complex of garishly painted stucco, pools, fountains, and white and blue tiles like in the TV movie we saw in Canterbury.

There was a little girl on the bus who looked like Cathy as a child, with blue eyes and freckles. She wordlessly showed me her doll and pointed to a button pinned to her sweater, "I am four years old."

As she and her mummy were leaving, the mum said, "Be careful, you're only wee. Go very straight. That's a big girl."

There were archeological digs here and there, though not in darling Chichester, where the fruit trees were heavily pregnant with bloom. There was a neat arched round thing in the middle of the street by Woolworth's, or "Woolies." The cathedral is being restored, but almost too late. The houses are all named, and one is called Noglands.

When we arrived in Portsmouth, the bus driver tried to tell us where to go.

He stopped at a street stop, and said, "Ask the bobby out there."

We asked for the coach station.

He, in his shirtsleeves, said, "Just under the RR, turn left, and it's just there, at the end of that street. It's a beautiful day for a walk..."

"Yes, but—" we started to say, but continued on, lugging our suitcases. After going several blocks to an underpass, we turned left and, in the distance, was some sort of building. We lugged on. But when a cab came, we hailed it. It must have been at least a mile, that "lovely walk."

We finally found the Info Center for National Coaches; it was well-manned or, womaned. A nice gal went over every coach schedule with us, but there would be no way to catch one unless we spent the night.

"Try a train," she suggested.

So, we went to the train station—only a couple of blocks' walk—but Jami wanted to get a taxi to the Tourist Info Center to get the route mapped first. We hailed one and were driven across town to the Sealink and Ferry Terminal, but the kiosk office was closed and wouldn't reopen for an hour.

We got another taxi to Dickens' house and were left alone since no one else was there. Four rooms were open and refurnished. The room he was born in had definite vibrations: others have "felt a presence," said the caretaker. In the bedroom opposite, there are cases of his desk things, letters, jewelry, drawings by the illustrators, a chair of his, and the chaise he died on— un-roped off. Jami took pictures of me on it. I felt no vibes there like I had in his bedroom.

The first floor had a living room and a dining room

with too-new paint and crystal mixed in with antiques, but it was otherwise tasteful. We couldn't go to the third floor, but it was fantastic nonetheless. There are houses next to it that are still lived in.

When we were going to call for a cab, the caretaker said, "What? Why the ferry station is just through there. Take this footpath to the main road and it is right there." We walked another mile, marveling at the hardy folk, and got to the Info Center at 1:05 p.m.—still closed. While we waited, we ordered beer and salad plates. The clerk arrived at 1:30 and perused the schedules, informing us that the chief Info Office was at the train/bus station we'd just taken the cab from, and found that there was no way to get to Stratford except by train through London. We gave up.

We took a cab back to the railroad station, bought tickets—this time to Waterloo for $26 more—left Portsmouth at 2:53 p.m., and arrived in London at 4:27 p.m. We found a bus to Bradford—full—but persevered and hailed a taxi to Nottingham with an arrival of 9:30 p.m. It was a lovely, warm, and sunny day. A Jamaican cab driver took us to the RR station, but an impatient clerk (all have been handsome) was not encouraging, so we asked a female constable (so many dozens of bobbies arrived as a football game let out) and she recommended the Victoria Hotel. The hotels by the RR station looked weird, but old and formerly elegant in a crummy part of town. Victoria was elegant—and another £23. It had a large double bed and a single; heating; a color TV; and a farmhouse breakfast of eggs, juice, fruit, bread, bacon, sausage, and black pudding. Good coffee. We took rolls.

Nottingham was huge and grim, and it rained this morning. Beyond the bus station next door: old stone mansions and behind those, stone ruins, terraces, and more forest—pines. Sign for a social club in a cinema building read "Eyes...down" and the time the show started. Poor viewing today: more grimy brick-stone houses, windows fogged up inside, and everything wet from Mansfield to Sheffield. I read a biography of Emily Dickinson en route to the next few towns.

We spread out in the back seats of local buses and pressed on. Our passes weren't as good, but persever-ance continued. We changed at Sheffield, which was full of outdoor sheds, but the cafeteria had great food and it was clean and warm. The bus stations are not like ours: few loiterers, if any, and everyone is so cheery and kind, though they look sour until spoken to. We get called "dearie," "luv," or "darlin'" everywhere we go.

Bradford

On the trail of the Brontës, we hopped on the local 665 bus. Bradford station was a surprise: big and organized with lower level concourse escalators. But the con-ductor spoke little English and since we couldn't un-derstand—or vice versa—we got off at the Info Center and walked back to town. It was still open and the clerk called the Black Bull Inn and booked us one of the five bedrooms. She called the town's one taxi and we were swept up onto the cobbled street as it rained.

We rang the doorbell there and, in time, Mr. Ben-nett came down and let us in, helping us to the back door and into our room at the head of the stairs, unsmiling and terse. He was a handsome man in his early 40s, who scooted his stockinged feet across the hall to his own quarters. The bathroom (shared by all, family too) and the stairs separated us. We noted the bar was well stocked and the artificial gas fire was going; there was also an enormous German shepherd dog. It henceforth occupied the landing during the day.

We opened our door to a pale-pink-flower wallpapered room that slanted downward toward the steep street below. It had two wooden beds, one higher than the other emphasizing the slant; the dresser so low, its mirror only showed you from feet to waist; a big TV; another false fireplace that ate ten pounds sterling; a recessed window with red, white, and grey flowered curtains; a mantel piece; an awful painting hung opposite a too-small glass ship; a sink with two pink and white hand towels; one large orange bath towel on a hook; and a mirror too high to see anything but the top of your head. Large lavender and navy flowers with green leaves sit atop a wood-veneered wardrobe. Beige carpet. The white chenille bedspreads were a relief, though lots of heavy blankets forewarned us. All of its oddities added to our fun, and nowhere did we have better food than in the dining room.

The bar was deserted all afternoon and we wondered at its non-attendance, except for the dog. We put more sweaters on and went outside to explore surroundings. All the shops were closed except one book store where we bought Charlotte Brontë's early works and Daphne de Maurier's *The Infernal World of Bran-*

well Brontë. The Brontë museum at the Parsonage was very well done. There was little of Emily, but we noted her view from the window in her tiny room. A hodge-podge of green-mossed and grey tombstones lay between her, the rugged church, and the walled-in fields beyond.

Back at the hotel, we asked a lad if they served dinner. He said, "Yes, at 7:00," so at that hour we descended the stairs to see the bar filling with people. We were drinking gin and tonics when a darling little round grey-haired lady gave us the dinner menu with her broken wrist. We ordered venison, guinea fowl, three fresh veggies, two potatoes, a huge salad with watercress sprouts, and a bottle of Mateus Rosé—wow!

After dinner at the pub that night, we had scotch and pints and talked to three Yorkshire lads. One was a lorry driver, one into furniture, and one was a WWII vet. They had to leave at 10:30; only residents can continue drinking at night. They were resigned to it and told us funny stories about drunk driving laws. We went to bed early after deciding to stay another night.

26,400 + 10,000 + 9,400 + 18,600 + 123,000 = 187,400

$230 train transfer to Paris

We were "knocked up" for breakfast at 9:00: eggs, fried bread, bacon, sausage, and tomato for me, while Jami had pork and beans on toast with an egg! Toast with Dundee [marmalade], of course, and coffee. We returned to the Info Center for future bus schedules, bought a book about the Brontës and while Kathy, the clerk, wrapped it for us, she told us about her family in Haworth. When I asked if she was interested in [the

Brontës], she said, "The Brontës weren't the only family with tragedies."

Still, "My great-grandfather was the town barber and cut their hair" was a fact that gave her pride. She had the physiognomy of a rag doll: a boneless face, soft and settling into chin, and tight sleeves that appeared stuffed. We wondered if the Brontë girls might have been similarly built. Then, next door at the post office, the terse postmaster had me undo some of Kathy's tape and replace it with a few pieces of string so I could send it book rate. I filled in all the forms, stuck on stamps, and tossed it into the bag. Cost: £1.18 We also bought three sheep skins that we spotted on our walk up the hill (lamb) for £7 ($14) each, plus £1.50 ($3) for shipping. £26 total.

For lunch, we ordered a "nutty whole meal cob" (a cob being a loaf of bread), cheese, milk, fruit, mayo, and watercress sprouts before setting off for the moors. The sun had earlier threatened a time or two, but the day rapidly became misty and rainy. We took pictures in the graveyard, in pastures with horses and on a path full of puddles and slippery black earth. The brisk wind howled as we reached the moors. When we stepped away from the shelter of the stone wall, I could lean against it. Everywhere sheep and lambs.

We stopped on a sheltered bench and ate our delicious repast, or part of it, saving the milk and fruit. Our mouths were full of rain. Our wet hair whipped about our heads. I laughed at my usual drowned-rat appearance. Our shoes were wet, but not cold. Our "thin skins" kept us warm. But Oh, my ears!

We passed an abandoned farm house that looked like my idea of Top Withens, the inspiration for the house in Wuthering Heights, and got as far as the falls. Ahead of us stretched endless sodden and windy moors. We decided the pictures of my Top Withens were enough and I was of the opinion that even frail Emily would not have walked that far, when there were so many other similar houses nearer. So, we turned back and climbed over the brown about-to-bloom heather amongst the long-haired sheep and lambs. The wind behind us made our return easy, though our shoes were soggy and stained with black mud.

On our way back to the hotel, we changed buses at Keighley and I read a new magazine with the best article yet. In the room, Jami bathed as I set my hair before going downstairs for another great meal: a beef steak, a ham steak with pineapple, a pork steak with whole mushrooms, a big piece of liver, a fried egg, lettuce, tomatoes and cucumbers, and sausage. On the side: fresh whole baby carrots, zucchini, and round fried potatoes—whew! Jami had pork in marsala and cream. White wine. After eating, we went into the pub and ordered the cider the three young men had told us about. A man tried to engage Jami in conversation, but we sat apart from him; we were so tired and warm and sleepy.

The next morning, we ate breakfast at 8:00 and walked down to Changegate. A nice lady helped us find the bus. It was lovely country: more rock fences snaking up green pastures full of sheep, stately stone houses, stone villages, stone bridges, and more trees. The air was thick with fog for part of the journey. However,

Kendal was large and getting touristy, as was Windermere.

In the rain, the lake looked like a slab of polished slate, with ridges. We saw more pines, woods, and fields of peach-colored heather. But I'm not too impressed with Keswick; it is large and busy, more so than what we've seen elsewhere. A man at the bus station was rude and unhelpful.

We had lunch of "John Peale Pie" (pheasant), two small baked (jacket) potatoes, a large green salad with lots of green peppers, and wine, all for £1.50.

We walked all over trying to find the Info Station, but signs led us around in a circle. We resigned to take the local bus to Carlisle and needed a bank, but none were open. Using our heads, we read the info book and saw that there were different kinds of information stations: national, regional, and local. Oh. We were sent to a Scottish bus line station and an inspector told us all we needed to know: the bus for Ayr was in front of us, but full, so we were escorted onto another while the other bus would wait for us at the next stop. There was a hamster on the bus due to an incident in Carlisle.

France

Le Premier Temps
What a lovely spring landscape that afternoon and
     night in Lourdes.
Remember:
train seats and headrests
the dark tobacco smell
sudden ticket puncher
sassy Spanish rock n' roll
views of Mediterranean villages
vineyards circling the Pyrenees
ancient nucleus inland, French farms
La Residence du Champ de Mars

We arrived in Paris at twelve and met our friend,
Wendy. We stood in the queue for an hour and a half
for a taxi; the drive was a fury and the woman at the
wheel kept pointing out sights as they flashed by. Our
room is adorable with flowered wallpaper tiles, a gable window, slanted closet, and quilts. A separate entry
room with its own sink, shower, and bidet, with the toilette across the hall. I climbed the slanted bed and tried
to get some sleep, but it was cold. The peak of the Eiffel
Tower is visible from our sixth-floor window.

Upon waking, I discovered I'd goofed on the dates
and that we had only one day in the city. Still, we found
the bank, tabac with stamps, and pharmacie all in an
adjacent block on Rue de Basque. We set out in a taxi
to buy tickets via hovercraft to London before being
dropped off at the Louvre to see as many paintings as
possible from 11:00 a.m. to 2:00 p.m. Then we wandered through the fabulous Notre Dame and lit candles. It snowed as we took pictures by the Jeanne d'Arc

statue. The stained-glass windows were unbelievable. We ate lunch across the street: Boeuf Bourguignon, mushrooms (cold), rosé, French-fried potatoes, ice cream, and coffee.

We couldn't find the church on Île St. Louis, but were shown in by a girl after asking a local. It was charming in white and gold with small simple paintings. Jack Kerouac was baptized at the St. Louis sister church in Lowell, Massachusetts. I lit a candle for him in front of Mary's statue, sat, and meditated awhile. There was only one other small group inside, and at first, I found their French annoying, but then realized it added to the effect.

The sun was shining as we walked across the bridge and took pictures of ourselves with Notre Dame in the background. The banks were closed and we were out of money, so we went back to our room to crunch some numbers. The snow revived and we had no heat in our radiator. Seventy-year-old men and women were dressed in full mountain-climbing regalia—knee socks, boots, and backpacks—in La Land du Nord.

On the train
Northern French narrow tall houses
Steep-pitched roofs and gables
Variegated gingerbread trim and chimneys
Hansel and Gretel cottages in bucolic countryside
Clear dawn days, orange trees
Compartment seats open to a window
Draft down neck, stiff seats, but we
are two, facing all, alone

Italia: "Getting our sea legs"

On our ferry to Italy from Spain, a guy hung over our table as we played cribbage. He said something.

I answered, "Je ne sais pas," telling Jami it wasn't as exciting in English.

She said, "Is 'Duh' more exact?"

We talked about the ferry's waterbeds, the merry-go-round, the icy water, sharks. We thought of its squishy seats, comfortable chairs, and glass tables.

We sweated for a minute when we saw a man in a cabin with two bunks (two more out of sight), thinking we'd paid for an outside cabin for two, and accosted the purser to clear it up. We thought we had been put in a quadruple for 4,000 lira, but had paid 5,500 for a double, so we accosted a second purser. He finally made us understand that a "quad" meant four people in a cabin. We shut up, since our room was so tiny even we two couldn't move without one climbing in the bunk.

Still, the porthole's extra space should mean something. Where was our guardian angel? On second thought, we speculated it might be too bloody cold in an outside cabin since we were just barely warm as it was. As we sat in the lounge, Jami was concerned about a family we were taking seats from with five kids.

The sea was rough and smashed against the port windows. A little five-year-old from an affectionate family squealed—he was showing off for me. We closed the brown-and-white blinds, watched a Spanish movie, and napped before visiting the self-service restaurant: paella, fish, salad, and wine. Public transportation here has terrific food. We saw the Spanish scarf we'd searched all over Spain for in the display case. The clerk wasn't interested—he wouldn't take lira and we'd spent all of our pesetas. I said I could come back in the morning, but he never reopened.

I found I loved the motion and didn't need to take anti-nausea pills. It's amazing to be behind the breakers. The windows were too wet for pictures, so we drank gin and tonics, played cribbage, and lunged. The French Connection would be shown, but that night we went to bed instead and slept like babies.

We woke up at 8:00 a.m. (time change, 9:00 a.m.) for docking in Genoa. We presented our passports to Customs, but we didn't clear. Our taxi driver worried about soldiers stopping our cab (it turned out OK.) Instead, we went to the railroad station and I thought of Dickens' Italian villa somewhere up there. Nice station—Italy. We got tickets to Firenze and had cappuccino. There was a bug in my first cup, but I braved another.

When we arrived in Firenze, we grabbed a phone booth—which took tokens only—and dropped our luggage. I tried to get Wesley and Shirley, friends from Saratoga, to meet us in 15 minutes. Half an hour later, they appeared and we were taken to great martinis and cheer in their small apartment. The Italian countryside with views of Florence. But there were water restrictions. Pressure.

The next day, we toured the Duomo, Accademia (Davido), Uffizi (after Fiesole), and Santa Croce where Dante, Michelangelo, Galileo, and Rossini are buried.

We visited a church and heard an organ play, at last. We ate great pizza in Fiesole and Shirley showed us their former villa with a view of valley. We went to the "Blue Bar" for strawberries and cream and noticed a disco for kids in the basement. The teenagers were all smoking. Ghi [a friend] reminisced about her home. She also told us that school dances provide cases of wine; boys get sick and no one dances.

On Monday, Shirley drove us to Siena in the afternoon after the All-Italy handcraft show. I bought gifts and a tray that I then had to carry. I wasn't up on my Siena, excepting the marvelous church and museum, so we bought guides. The Square hosts medieval horse races on July 2 and August 16. There were wonderful ancient streets and Jami and Ghi climbed 360 steps to a tower across slanted streets. [A cross] marks the spot. We drank more cappuccino and ate pastries on the long drive back. We saw much, but no Leonardo!

Even though we had bought our reservations in advance, when we got on the train, we didn't have tickets! The conductor was pissed. We said, "OK, now what?" While Shirley had loaned us 10,000 lira, we could only pay our way to Bologna. We dashed off, barely able to get a traveler's check cashed and hopped back on to Milano. From there, we bought tickets to Paris—$230 all told. An American from Napa helped us while his Italian wife explained our problem to the second conductor, who thought it was hilarious. Odd seating arrangement. No lunch.

On the train to Paris
Ham salad and wine at 2:00

Beautiful black woman in Switzerland
Italians indifferent
Hooray for France, streets, cars, pedestrians
Directions, arrows: ← ↑ ⟳

London

We checked into the Alison House Hotel and went to a picturesque pub, but it was too full of loud rock 'n roll. We ate at The Tent before bed, which was excellent, but $12. On Friday morning, we got "Coach Master Pass" bus tickets at Victoria station and signed up for a two-hour tour to fit in before visiting Queen's Gallery, the National Gallery, Trafalgar Square, the National Portrait Gallery, the British Museum—King Edward VIII—and Great Russell Street. Called Jay.

My interview for *Honey Magazine* was scheduled for 7:30 p.m. with Minty. Wine shop across the street—had bought wine already, but didn't have dinner.

Saturday Itinerary
Buckingham Palace, Changing of the Guard,
    Victoria and Albert Museum
Treasures of Prints Room
Royal Portrait Gallery
Hampton Court
Costume Museum
Art and flowers
Chapter House
Westminster Abbey
Eat. Tea and wine at Landesman's (Stewart Hogarth).
"The Crucible of Blood" at Haymarket

"The Mousetrap" at St. Martins

We walked to Sherlock Holmes' Baker Street and talked to a waitress at the Duke of Buckingham Pub, which had lovely antique décor. American rock 'n roll played as the bitters, ale, and gin settled in. Hot, stuffy, noisy, friendly.

We met a great guide on a Charles Dickens walking tour who stood on tiptoes. Embankment Underground: saw river gate place where a blocking factory was (it never moved), rookeries, arches to which Dickens referred in his books... Duke of Buckingham's palace. Then to Adelphi section: buildings still there—Pepys' home—houses with torch snuffers, more rookeries and slums. Went to Rules Restaurant (36 Maiden Lane) where Dickens went. Saw Peabody's slum clearance buildings. We were thrilled to finally see Covent Garden, home of our favorite ballet company, The Royal Ballet. Noted Adam's architecture where buildings appear laced at the seams.

At a late opera gala, Prince Michael of Kent (the Queen's nephew) sat close to us during dress rehearsal. It was a wonderful show, though we waited for the prince for an hour and a half outside, hoping to catch a ride. We then couldn't get a cab and more than two hours passed before we decided to just walk home. We spotted the Prince's car at Buckingham Palace. We had a "pint" of bitters in the Duke of Edinburgh Pub where a nice young man explained the mug he was holding, but I couldn't hear, and coughed until 4:30 a.m.

On Sunday morning, we left the house at ten and went to Victoria Station to find out if they had a schedule of English buses. The clerk said we actually had to go to Victoria Coach Station (VCS) and several hours later, I realized "buses" meant city and "coaches" meant long distance. So, we walked the two blocks to VCS and queued up again. A little man told us to go to the Green Line booth we'd already passed for coaches to Gravesend. As we queued up at the Green Line, a man there said that they had no service to Gravesend. We told him that the sign in front read "Book Anywhere in England." He showed us a round-about way we could go but informed us, "Only trains go to Gravesend."

We walked back to VCS and checked our baggage before realizing we didn't need to, and queued up to get first-class train tickets to Gravesend. The man there told us we were still at the wrong station and had to get that specific train at Charing Cross. At that point, we decided to forget Gravesend and head to Rochester.

When we went back to the Green Line man to queue up, I said, "OK, we'll do it your way and go to Rochester."

"No," he said. "The Green Line only goes within a 30-mile radius of London, not as far as Rochester."

"So, what about your sign for 'National Express?'" I asked.

"Can't handle Coach Master lanes here. Go back to VCS," he replied.

Back again to our old friend at the VCS queue. He gave us the time of bus and nicely remarked that we should check if they had a seat for us "over there."

We queued up for the reservation window and finally got the seats and passes validated—eureka! It had taken one and a half hours to do *this* tour. No fish and chips yet. Sign on every street corner: "LOOK RIGHT →"

Lisbon, Portugal

From the plane
Circumscribed cumulus clouds
against the shadow of our plane encircled
by a rainbow orb. Beneath, the neat new green
fields,
red earth dotted with clusters of red-roofed white
houses,
splashes of sandstone cliffs, a birthmark forest
and the broad yellow Tagus River,
washing hanging from every window on long lines.

—

Guarda
Cactus on table as flower
French girl in shop tries to help
a town with restaurant and public square
All the housing on stilts
Why?
Driver gives Phillipe signs
Stone walls around fields
An obelisk.

—

In Albufeira, Portugal, we found a super new high-rise hotel—450 rooms—far from the village and beach. We drove through fig and orange orchards on an old country road to get to the manor, a severe white thing. Hove into the one-year old mammoth Montechoro Hotel where Hella had been the first guest. She told us of the electricity failure there, how the elevators quit earlier, and that the baggage didn't arrive. The dining room is like a mess hall, huge and noisy with no atmosphere. The water pressure varies as does the hot water. One sink stopped up. Toilet seat of cheapest plastic. In another year, it'll be a slum.

Our room is large and sparsely furnished in a modern style with a glass table and overstuffed chairs in white, grey, and fuchsia. But the marble-topped bath with two basins isn't working. There's a flimsy shower curtain to no effect. One ashtray in the whole place, one crooked picture in the hallway next to older master drawings: bits of Bosch beautifully framed, either antique or copies. Ultra-modern steel lights frame the beds. The balcony has a white wall and white, plastic chairs. It would have been good for sunbathing if it hadn't been raining, though I suspected it would be hot and the view obscured. Cheap; not the Ritz. The room was the biggest, but without charm, no "home."

I'm complaining? Well, by now we're spoiled. I criticize taste and motives. Again, the plumbing is a catastrophic noise! We took pictures off the balcony, even though surrounded by fog.

Later, we saw *Maggie Cassidy* on an English book rack outside a café in Faro where Hella made a stop earlier to show us the square and the harbor. Lots of young internationals.

Meals

Three times a day
plus two breaks eating with others we're

forced into conversation with, there's interest,
but three to five days of this?
We can't wait to eat and get on
Each meal
Modern light switches

I resent this plastic monument to greed defacing
the charming village. Below us are new structures quite
in keeping with the original of the town; this has been
possible since the revolution. Hotel full of families and
darling children.

Breakfast was a sick display of cold cuts and dubious fruits. No oranges. There were dozens of waiters,
but it took forever to get coffee. Pastries inferior. Hella informed us that the Sun City diplomat, Hazel, is ill
with dysentery.

We were bundled up when our bus arrived in the
village, since it showered earlier. We left our wash
on the balcony, and in town the sun came out as we
weaved our way aimlessly through the narrow, cobbled
streets among other tourists until I bought a book with
a map. It was difficult to figure out, but we followed it
to a recommended "rustic" restaurant, though the rest
of the group wanted a more elegant one.

Winding, climbing, plunging little streets with the
sidewalks a foot wide. Tiny cars and motorcycles zipping along the small street. We persevered up, around,
and down and found the Ruína Restaurant five minutes
before it opened. The bar on the upper level had a balcony overlooking the bay and the beach was jammed
with fishing boats, fishermen, fish drying in sun, trucks,
and nets. We were directed down a long, curving flight

of stairs to the restaurant.

There, a double-decker case held all kinds of raw fish; on top were salads, fried fish, and shrimp. There was also an enormous pot of steaming bouillabaisse. We picked our own fish, which the attendant then took out and over to the cook at the next counter who sliced it open and put it on the grill. Jami and I chose tuna salads replete with vegetables, lettuce, and the bouillabaisse, longingly eyeing the clams, sardines, sole, and bass.

But our choice was too filling anyway what with the wine and fresh grainy bread—best we've had: both the salad dressing and the soup needed mopping with it. Every kind of fish. The bouillabaisse: whole sardines and great chunks of the others, plus vegetables, completely satisfying. The Atlantic crashed on the beach below.

Hella appeared, meeting Phillipe and his son, who turned out to be tall and mustached! We went to the bar terrace to drink port outside—perfectly lovely. Our only disappointment was our determination to speak Portuguese, but everyone spoke English! After baking ourselves, we walked down narrow steps to the beach and among the boats, picked up rocks and shells, and smiled at the charging water. Later, back up and into the narrow, bumpy streets and down into the square, we bought oranges at the market; wine, cheese, chocolate, and yogurt in the grocery store. A big bottle of sparkling Lancers cost 96 escudos, or two dollars.

We hopped back on the bus hoping to sunbathe at the hotel, but our balcony was covered in shade. Still, our clothes were dry and safe. We also bought stamps at the post office—a store open during siesta! A lovely, lovely day. Wonderful people. Jami and I played cribbage and napped without a schedule. During the bus ride, our friend Sue said she didn't like this town too much and hated places catering to tourists. Jami and I laughed together because Sue only wanted to shop and loved the big shopping places—a total tourist. She bought three tablecloths here (ugh) whereas Jami and I always tried to avoid shops and the tourists.

The room was like a hospital one, but we were happy. The music on the radio was a mixture of everything, with a little too much American rock or funk.

Sagres

The Lighthouse is the sleeping place of the
    goddesses

No one dared go at night

We climbed to the prism, two bulbs

3,000 watts, 60 miles for airplanes

Protected courtyards, no plants, warm São Vicente

Southwest corner of Europe, Henrique the
    Navigator

spent forty years at the fort

Phillipe is driving fast

Primary school cupola

Stray Thoughts

Aljezur was a pretty village, old wall, most popular tour, north of the ocean, village pines eucalyptus. Zambujeira, all trip scenery terrific. Casa Branca view toward the sea; land confiscated by communists. (Mostly state-owned, perhaps.) Vasco de Gama was born at the Sines resort. Santiago de Cacém for lunch, roof of four levels. Story of a stork: a little boy wanted a little brother. Why didn't you tell the bird you wanted one? A woman and St. Peter, no, wrong, used to be an angel word, no, a chicken. A W.C. and an English lady in Switzerland are looking for a room. Khrushchev and Kennedy telephone a bell, it cost $101.

—

On our way to Lisbon, we saw cork oak forests, then flat land, and then pines. Everything was sandy like in Pacific Grove and Michigan. Outside, there were fluffy clouds in the blue sky. All of Portugal was a park—any park, all parks! We went to Alcazar du Sol for port and pine candy and saw TV antennae everywhere. But, SABENA airline was such a bloody experience (never again)!

Our friend Phillipe decided to drive us "home." We stopped for cork, rock roses, and wild flowers outside of Sol. He ran out of the car and carved off a piece of cork from the forest that we kept. Setúbal was communist, industrial, busy, dirty, pretty. There was a depressive mood.

The hotel was adequate, even though it was five stars. The room was small, but everything worked. I had an awful cold, Jami a sore throat with white spots and a sore tongue. Despite that, we took off, went to Avenida da Liberdade, and walked down the boulevard to the railroad station. The façade is a great example of the intricate Manueline architectural style. Groups of men stood in the street discussing politics (I presume).

Alberto was sad about changes to his city: "Many are unemployed here, but not on welfare. U.S. money is spent on salaries for managers of the southern agricultural reform, which isn't making any money. The best schools are run by the nuns and monks who aren't allowed to live in the local communities."

Alberto showed us the Jerónimos Monastery, now empty and used only for occasional concerts. He took us to Alfama, which was a lot like Casbah: dirty with garbage and dog shit under stands of fish, live snails, vegetables and fruit. Beggars on the streets included little children, some of whom were deformed. Black Horse Square and the other monuments were unkempt.

The fado place, like the flamenco, was for tourists. Jami and I decided to go anyway and were anesthetized and happy. She got a haircut and looked adorable. We had huge oysters on shells like barnacles. The drive to Sintra was high and hilly and from Cascais to Estoril it poured rain.

Rossio Square
Shopping.
Buses #2, 3, and 4: five escudos.
Flowers.
All streets go to the river,
to Black Horse Square.
Tile factory, Santa Ana, taxi.

Shipping and shopping near our hotel.
Casal Mendes.
Folklore Pop Art.
Ferry boats across river.
Castle St. George missed.
Rain.
Fancy new houses, old ruins.
Didn't visit any palaces, though tried for a kitchen.
Too many tourists—a holiday
—

We drove over what must have been gorgeous shoreline, but the windows were so wet that the breakers looked like rick-rack. The rain drowned a small car; its angry little horn complained for minutes. Jami and I tried to find American Express and a Tourism Office. We skipped our venture downtown and got all mixed up, having been given the wrong directions. Instead, we had port at a café before starting back.

We just happened to look up to find the Tourism Office we'd been looking for. Bank of America changed our money; all of the other banks were closed. The [clerk] had us into a new hotel and half way out of Portugal in minutes. The directions Hella gave us were slipping. We tried to check with her Friday afternoon, but the lines were busy and there was too much rain, so we had to stay over on Monday. Still, all so much simpler than we feared—great relief.

During the gala dinner, we got group pictures and exchanged addresses (Jami began passing them around). Everyone was so nice and sad under a big, full moon. We were on the top floor, which didn't help our colds. We had cream of asparagus soup, Coquille St. Jacques, a real steak, some frozen dessert, and two kinds of wine. Freedom now! [She and Jami would depart from their tour group and venture off as a twosome.]

On Saturday morning, we called the Diplomático and they said our rooms would be ready when we were. We had a huge breakfast in the room, packed, and were out of the Altis by 10:30. We've been tipping too much in fear, even though it says service included. Ah well. The Diplomático hotel was nice, if not elegant. It was homier with decorative tile in the bedroom, a massage [device] on the bed, a dressing room bigger than Altis, a balcony, a royal blue carpet, and flowered wallpaper with white rock roses on a mustard ground. There were red and blue dots on the water faucets, room radios, and elevators. The staff was relaxed and friendly. There was also a nice little gift shop, bar, and restaurant with a coffee shop—fast service.

We hadn't yet investigated before going to the market a half-block up to buy gin, wine, tonic, soap, bread, and lime. They gave us a transparent plastic bag, so we stopped across the street in a shopping and shipping store (open Sunday and Monday!). I got a shopping bag woven with basket handles in dark green and white with a rooster and red and orange accents. We put the groceries in it and walked to the farmacía around the corner to buy cough medicine, Kleenex, and cream rinse, forgetting the aspirin and Listerine for which we'd gone. Later, we packed a black bag full of clothes and shipped it home, leaving only two change options. So be it.

Showers and sun alternated as we walked back at 12:30 p.m. and got into bed with gin and tonic, bread and cheese, and figs. We were feeling poorly (head and throat, which turned into a day's pneumonia for me) but much happier on our own. Everyone was helpful and nice, and I hoped to feel up to a service and more sightseeing soon.

Marvelous monuments and empty palaces with beggars and filth made no sense. Alberto, our tour guide, said that many of the professionals—doctors and lawyers—moved to Brazil. Health note: my fingernails are disintegrating and breaking before they reach the end of each finger—scaly, flaking, awful. Why? Never so much bread and pastry. Not enough protein and greens? Must take vitamin pills, eat eggs, fish, and meat... Jami's OK. Why me?

I'd like to walk to the top
of that furry hill to see a golden path,
five trees huddled on a crest, properly arranged.
What would be on top? Only me, expanded.

—

Miserable with the cold, so I couldn't get out to look at the Portuguese sky. It is all one world, we are all God's children; OK, so the same sky may be over California, but those fluffy white clouds are Portuguese, and Lisbon's alone. That crooked moon last night the same moon, yes, but with a Portuguese slant. Don't argue. Sudden shafts of golden sun, though it showered continually. There must be a land of rainbows somewhere beyond the square buildings that face us.

Oh yes, the lamp posts! Last night in the nine-story

restaurant, we looked down on them and on our little street; galleons perched atop. Little crows on the side streets, but Castilho Street had the galleons.

Remember:

Men setting tile on Avenida da Liberdade scratching their heads

Piles of rubble

Looking down from my balcony, I see the sidewalks (White, grey, black)

Old men sit amidst the traffic,

hacking away at the stone to get them into shape

Every street made by hand

No camera

—

The American Express was a total bust. The clerk said simply that there were no buses traveling north to Madrid. We were booked at a Pousada near Aveiro with no idea how to get there. Take a train to Aveiro, then what? No one would talk about Spain. [Portuguese Pousadas and Spanish Paradors are government-owned accommodations in renovated historic buildings such as convents, monasteries, castles, and fortresses.]

We took a train ride from Lisbon and saw beautiful rich farms of eucalyptus, vineyards, fields, oaks, and cattle grazing by ruined walls. We spent the night in Pousada da Ria before driving into Aveiro; what a magnificent example of all that we love about Portugal. A nice older taxi driver took us to Tourismo and served as interpreter until we learned how to get to the inn.

We drove through charming villages with new tile houses, decorated with lots of oxen with yokes. Everything was richly folkloric but passed by so quickly that no pictures were possible. At the inn, fishing occurs right outside of our window in colorful boats. Though we were damp and cold (no heat), we ate another excellent three-course dinner and went to bed at 9:00 p.m. piled high with blankets.

For breakfast, we drank big cups of coffee and took a taxi over "pavimento undulate." The bay was like glass reflecting the Phoenician boats. The sandy dunes were flat like Glen Lake. We nearly missed the train since it arrived earlier than in our schedules. The station master and ticket seller both started yelling at us and whooshed us aboard where we were able to absorb more quaint farms and vistas of the sand and pounding Atlantic.

At Oporto, we crossed a horrendous bridge and stopped. We didn't know if we should get off, but a fellow passenger took pity on us and said "Not yet." We backed across the bridge again and when the train stopped, he said, "Now." We tried to check our luggage, but there were no such lockers even though there was a sign. I drew pictures for an Information Officer who couldn't speak English. Jami and I hauled our bags and crossed a forked street twice before hailing a cab, but the driver told us that the Tourismo Office was just up the road and the ride would be too short.

As we walked uphill, our bags got heavier and heavier and I was feeling particularly rotten. We finally found the American Express, and of course, it was closed. It was only 1:00 p.m., so we sat on the step until 2:30 p.m. A nice young man then sold us train tickets straight to San Sebastián: 4 p.m. until 4 p.m. the next day! 24 hours on coach and a day late. We were told to stay in Hotel Batalha that overlooked the station and is beyond description. Jami handed the address of the hotel to a woman selling strawberries and asked for directions. The woman couldn't read English though, and thought Jami was begging and gave her a coin. We lost a few days trying to get out of Portugal along the scratched, cold, foggy coast.

Remember:

Faucets take four turns to work.

Towels harsh.

Ceramic tile in all but linoleum floors.

Emergency cord in shower.

Jami and I cleared out of our room by noon (I washed my hair), stowed our bags in the lobby, and went to the farmacía and market. We decided not to buy wine, crackers, cheese, and juice; but tea, water, and two oranges instead. I was hoping to force liquids since I couldn't shake the bug; I had taken too much cough medicine and was experiencing vertigo and muscle spasms without much sleep. My mouth was so dry it tasted of salt and my temples were splitting.

Views of Oporto from the four-cornered windows were like "find the face" pictures—every time we looked, we saw something different: aqueducts, churches, vacant lots above busy streets, incredible slums with new additions, dogs, cats, goats. The radio reception was poor; we tuned to classical, jazz, or country and got either only bass or melody. Drinks were double what they were only two months ago: $4 each for gin!

Spain

Ciudad Rodrigo y Madrid
Parador palace, ancient Moorish fortress,
Roman aqueduct, table-top plateau, billboards, gas
    stations,
stone, oaks, cattle lands, El Corte Inglés, Galerías
    Preciados,
Salamanca American bar: "St. Louis Woman,"
    "Lola," "Jezebel"
Black olives taste like sour oil
Extensive selection of paperbacks: whole rack of
    Agatha Christie, Erica Jong, David Copperfield
Shakespeare and Sylvester Stallone
1,800 royal rooms
Geographical center of Iberian Peninsula
—

(Corte Inglés is a big chain department store, except no medicine is sold anywhere but in farmacías. Not even aspirin or cough drops (but makeup, soap, and Kleenex—OK). Clothes upstairs: men on one floor, women and children another. Records, tapes, automotive supplies, postcards, baskets, handcrafts, junk, souvenirs—the works. The local movie theaters show last year's films, though some new to me (but not to Jami). Music on the radio largely English and American rock stars—imitators of old chestnuts, pop and classic.)

In Escorial, Hella demonstrated the acoustics in a room near the court entrance by whispering in one corner and facing a wall, and we could hear her perfectly in the opposite corner. We noted the double-headed eagle of Hapsburgs and the oldest gate in Spain with an escutcheon on it. We lunched in Toledo, viewed Hostal del Cardenal and the suckling pigs, and took pictures of El Greco and Judas trees. El Greco used only white, black, ochre, and for red, [rumor has it] the blood of pigeons. Diego Velázquez used sand from the Tagus River. The railroad station had Mudéjar architecture. La Mancha is "The Spot" with old olive trees, pointed base wine jugs, a blue fortress on a hill, and a village with one church. It also has the best cheese: queso Mancheco.

In Consuegra, the windmills were in ruins
The Order of St. Joan of the Cross
was supposedly founded here;
Cervantes was a tax collector
and imprisoned several times.
Saffron and purple crocus
Irrigation done by donkey and wheel,
Cave dwellers and pasodobles (bull fights)
Typical dish is La Mancha Pisto served in a jug with
    wooden spoons
like ratatouille.
Groves of olives
Villarta=wine press
Vente (Inn) del Quixote
—

The End of May might be the best time for Spain. There is always a dramatic sky with dots of windowless houses or ruins; distant villages, cities, and fields are hit by shafts of light in vast landscapes of green and red. We stayed in the only motel around and saw Gregory

Peck speak Spanish on TV.

It's election time and police with submachine guns patrolled the city. Every wall and lamp post is splattered with posters and on Saturday night, the streets were littered with fliers and parades. Our guide Pepe said he was going to vote for the Socialists because they planned to do wonderful things for Madrid like make it a seaport! Christmas is said to be a day to be happy here: no trees, just getting drunk.

Stopped in Santa Elena, our first Andalusian village. We saw lots of straw, pottery, and jamón (air-cured ham), and continued on to La Luisiana and La Carlota, which were founded in the 18th century by a Spanish king who colonized the area; he named them for his daughters. Germans were brought in.

During the bus rides, Jami and I sat in front doing isometric exercises for our tension. The bus seemed to always drive in the wrong lane. Narrow streets kept us cool. There were racks of pottery by the roadside and we were told that women paint the houses white each year after it rains. We learned about Bailén ceramic style brickwork, battles between Warburton and the French, and Andujar pots. Fields of limas and artichokes passed by. Eucalyptus, cypress. Gypsies originally from India. Old Moorish village with wall. Beautiful farms en route to Córdoba: cattle ranches, a few fruit trees below, and some "new" villages; white splashes in the bright green fields.

In Seneca's native land, Córdoba, a six-acre Mosque-Cathedral—the Mezquita—combines a 13th century Christian church within a mosque built in 784.

It was a Muslim Mecca of the West one thousand years ago and important for olive oil, wine, cotton, leather, and silver filigree. Phoenicians had an old mill there in 700 BC. "Tower of the Bad Death" legend haunts the land.

Arrived in Córdoba at 12:30 p.m. Our hotel smelled only of exhaust, since there was no smog control on cars. A great staircase sucked it up from the street and into our room. Jami got the blind stuck on the window that overlooked a shaft between walls. We had time to play cribbage and though we went to bed early, we found it difficult to sleep. Too hot. We were up by the 4:30 a.m. sun and out the door by 8:00 a.m.

Spanish meals are now monotonous. I had meat I couldn't cut—like a slab of leather—and overcooked vegetables. Potatoes and desserts are always great, excepting the one apple tart that had a hair in its crust. (Ice cream good.)

Jami and I sat in front during an exquisite drive on an old road over mountains dotted with olive groves. We stopped for olive pickers before Baena, the village where we bought donkey bells and Amontillado sherry and a gypsy woman tried to sell her grandchild to Hella. I longed to see inside the white haciendas, the watch towers on top of mountains, the ruined castles, the clustered splashes of villages and miles of velvet fields. Garlic, olives, almonds. Breathtaking.

We then arrived at the foot of the Sierra Nevadas in Granada, which were spectacular. Our guide, Antonio, was kind of sloppy and conceited, but handsome. We strolled two hours through Alhambra, but dashed through the cathedral and Capilla Real where Isabel and Ferdinand are buried along with Juana la Loca, Philip the Fair, and their child, Michael. The organ inside was run by electricity. Granada was, in general, clean and cheerful. A Parador was recommended to us, but we had already spent too much on postcards, wine, and cigarettes.

Torremolinos

A tourist mecca, our hotel in Torremolinos was gorgeous with a tile court and two big pools. We were late to a party at Julie and Sue's, so we bought wine and cheese, but weren't able to eat dinner (again). Our room was by the Mediterranean, but the beach was blocked so we couldn't go for a walk.

The next morning, we took a ferry ride to Morocco. Hotel Reina Cristina in Algeciras: miniature golf, old house, antiques, lobby, library, art show. Unfortunately, we arrived after dark and left at dawn, so we couldn't enjoy it all.

Next, we drove through cattle lands in the fog. I was unable to take pictures of Gibraltar, but caught mountains, cork oaks, and little haciendas. We learned about a leader of mountain troops and the phrase, "The King had thrown an eye on her." We were in the corner of Europe, where the Mediterranean met the Atlantic.

"Big Little" lice on cacti sent to Persia to color carpets red. Lipstick has also been made from it—and Cleopatra used it—the cochinilla cactus louse. Only one family breeds it in Seville.

Caballeros and Señoritas: black hat, tight suit,

leather apron, bells on skirts. Cowboys. Bull fights. Young bulls, young men: novedades. No picadors. Rejoneadores: on horseback. Torear: to fool around with bull. Only two services in Spain start on time: church and bull fights.

On the way back to our hotel, we passed pirate forts with tennis courts, and an old wall built by Arabs (rebuilt by Christians). The White Horse was punctual as the masons—who don't start on time, but end on time. Punctual as a nail.

In Jerez, we visited bodegas, or wine cellars, that aren't cellars but old monasteries with high ceilings to help even the temperature. American white oaks make for barrels that are filled with "mother" wine that is never emptied, which guarantees flavor. There are special soils for the two types of grape—palomino—that produce sherry. A "smeller" will then test it. Seville had one of the richest provinces in the south with the most privately-owned ground.

In Barcelona, some of the buildings and art were left over from the International Exposition of 1929: a bust from "Marriage of Figaro," and "Barber of Seville."

Palm Sunday in Seville brought bells and archives of the Indies. There were six to eight processions and tile paintings on the walls of the Cathedral. As we walked through the alley, the temperature dropped and orange blossoms filled the air. We passed by the Maria Luisa Park, huge paintings of provinces, and the bridge over Rio Grande (Guadalquivir, or "al-wādi al-kabīr" in Arabic), fifteen miles from the ocean. A wedding was going on in the Chapel of Macarena. We saw two floats:

Pilate's judgment of Jesus and one of Mary. They were carried by 45 men; another 37 were responsible for only 10 horses.

Hairstyles: twisted braids, pearls in back, crown front. There were red roses, pearls, and gorgeous little chapels. The floats were for Good Friday. We were witness to one of the largest cathedrals in the world next to St. Peters in Rome and St. Paul's in London. Forty-seven chapels, pure Gothic. Transplendent wisteria and plum.

Lunch was delicious: gazpacho, three filets (veal, pork, beef), potatoes pan-browned, artichoke hearts, ravioli with fresh spinach and cheese sauce, and ice cream in the Hotel Luz Sevilla. After eating, it began to pour. The waiter said, "just a shower." We decided to take our chances at seeing the floats to get pictures and saw two beauties. Jami bought a carnation from a gypsy for $0.30. The Cathedral was a bit gloomy, but I got to chat about Catholicism.

Cemetery. Hadrian's palace. Went to Roman ruins in the mist.

It rained so hard the processions were cancelled. Thousands of chairs were strewn about the city and roads were blocked off. We went back to the hotel, listened to classical music and ate terrific food.

On Monday in Manzanilla, we listened to the story of Venus with wine while enjoying the scents of lemons and chamomile. We boarded a new ferry on an eight-hour trip on the way to Algarve. It's the only one that could carry the bus, owned by a wealthy man. He was not a very friendly man and may or may not bring the boat back to meet us. On the way to Algarve: broad plains, vineyards, truck farming, tile works, and little villages pass us by. There are brilliant colors: a patch of pink blossoms, fog, and patches of sun amidst olives and eucalyptus. We crossed the Rio Tinto on a Roman bridge above red water. There was a slight smell of paper mill and rotten vegetables.

Algarve
Algarve is a Western city.
Not as hot as Spain with characteristic chimneys,
and towels with mirrors to ward off evil spirits
on the heads of donkeys—an Arab tradition.
People are happier, express themselves through
    dancing,
Must be the blood
only reconquered in 1249
The '74 revolution means foreign money is now
    allowed.
Almond tree stories
"If they didn't die, they're still alive" legends.
Beach of three sisters
Three fountains
Three loaves of bread
Arab souls left; if you don't clear your plate,
it rains

The town of Niebla was a Moorish stronghold with a huge fortified perfect wall. Heard the story about the Roman bridge in Salamanca.

Books: Ramón Sender's *Carolus Rex* and H.V. Morton's *Stranger in Spain*.

We had a good lunch with wine in a new parador

atop a hill that overlooked the village of Ayamonte and the river Guadiana before rousing the rich yet unreliable drunk who runs the ferry. He made us wait an hour while he had his lunch. Another delay keeping us from early arrival at the hotel tonight. Rained hard on the way, clearing as we leave.

Back to Spain on our own, Jami and I hopped a cold, cold train. We could see our breath and rushed to breakfast. We went through the Pyrenees in a cold, grey fog in the land of revolutionaries.

Remember:
Maria's passport at the border
Inland farms like picture books
Chuggy train alarm heard every ten seconds
Nurseries for trees and shrubs
Fair-haired children

In Girona: tree-lined streets, old cathedral with moss-covered steps, plastic railroad station, squares with old monuments, and outdoor cafes. On these short runs, first class is a joke.

When discussing my illness and the hemisphere theory, I noticed my throat began to hurt again, and it hadn't in France. I said, "My throat hurts; I must be in Spain."

"That's a good title," Jami said, then asked, "When the moss grows on only one side of the tree, what does that mean?"

I replied, "Another good title."

We kept repeating, "Oh, Look!"

Barcelona

When we get off the train, nada. A tortuous walk brought us to a "vestibule" where I was able to change my francs for pesetas. We ate soup, salad, and tea before heading into the Info Office. Due to a convention in town, all of the hotels are full. We were told where to go for a ferry but it was suggested that we return after siesta.

We checked our bags in lockers and walked (and walked) to Ramblas. Then we walked some more to the Oriente Hotel: full. We tried a hotel agency and were told, "Not one room in all of Barcelona." There were hundreds of hostels and pensiones everywhere, but we were too squeamish; we avoided a specific one because all of the men in the lobby were unfriendly. We tried another, The Royal. "Yes," the concierge said, "It costs 3,000 pesetas." Our limit was two, but I said, "We'll take it," because we still had to collect our bags. I was made to pay in advance—$60 per night!

When we were let into our room after a trip to the Picasso Museum, we realized it was one they saved for suckers. It had a filthy rug and a view of the hole. Oh well, better than the park, though the price rankled. Only one night. In search of food, we spotted a Wimpy's. How good a hamburger sounded, but we were given old buns, no mayo, and for the first time, poor French fries. With beer, it came to $8.50. Barcelona is the most expensive place we've found.

Disappointed but full and undaunted, we returned to The Royal for bed by way of Ramblas with a stop at the fabulous San José market where we bought enormous pears and took pictures.

I looked again in the book stands for *Cuentos de la Alhambra* by Washington Irving to no avail.

The next morning, we had to make a big decision about whether or not to take a ferry that day or stay in Barcelona. We decided that if we found a room, we'd stay. We meant to check out Gaudi Hotel, but walked across the street to "Residio" and got a room for 2,000 pesetas no problem. Jolly English-speaking concierge in an old grand residence room with French windows and a balcony overlooking Ramblas. In our room were carved wooden bedsteads, chairs painted in red and silver, and a big maple in new leaf in view. We were so happy.

Next to the hotel was a travel agency where we booked ferry tickets and changed money. We walked to the Maritime Museum, which had fabulous medieval shipyards where Columbus' ship was built. There was a wonderful display as well as a full-scale replica—or possibly real—ship with oars from the 15th century. We studied it until the museum closed at 1:30 p.m. Next, we walked to the Costume Museum thinking it would be open late—wrong. We hunted food and found Amaya, a recommended Basque restaurant. Clean and cozy, we had soup, French fries, and lamb; the latter was more like veal fried in batter.

The jolly maître d' gave us an elevated table in back to see the touring dance troupe that was set to perform. I analyzed all the dancers and the star this time was fiery and vulgar, but still great. We stayed five-and-a-half hours and went down to the bar after the show to congratulate our favorite. I got the autograph of one male dancer and was sorry I passed by the other; we didn't like his schmaltz, but he was good. We walked home at 2:30 in the morning.

The Costume Museum was next to the Picasso Museum and housed clothing from the 15th to 19th centuries in an old palace building dating to the 1400s. We wanted to see earlier items but realized they would be too hard to find. After a cab ride to Montserrat mountains, we went to Pueblo Español hoping to buy a shawl and a comb. I did buy a dress for Anne M., but no luck on flamenco shawls. I got a chip for John Gourley from a tile store that was being restored (or renewed). I began to feel woozy.

We grabbed paella for lunch and, during a rain shower, hailed a cab to Gaudi Park. I was feeling nauseated and chilled. We looked for a restroom, but the Museo was closed. It took ages to get back to our hotel, where I collapsed for two or three hours.

When I awoke the next morning, I felt a bit better, so we dressed and walked to the Opera House Liceo. Such fun! The day before, I babbled at a lady at what I thought was the ticket window while Jami hunted "seating" in the dictionary. The lady finally got through to me we were at the wrong window. We found the right one with a "mapa" of the theater and picked our seats. The theater had the best acoustics of any opera house in the world. Fascinating old boxed seats faced backwards. Even though I had to go straight to the bar to get water upon arriving at the opera, I enjoyed the performance and we walked home at midnight.

We re-packed in the morning, dressed, had breakfast, and caught a cab to the wharf where we waited over an hour to board. We were disappointed when we got inside the cabin, but at least it was a cabin. We ate more paella in the café and sat in squishy seats at the prow overlooking the Riviera.

Iberians say "Jesús" when you sneeze.

End of Spain.

Adiós.

Switzerland

In Switzerland, Greige patchwork fields filled the mountain sides. Fuzzy trees of forest green and leather-like mauve rivulets against the rock; finger thrusts of snow reached down on the peaks amid a row of fluffy orange and chartreuse. Hang gliders looked like kites or birds. Heidi houses were high on the meadows. Red and yellow tulips hung against grey walls. How to get there? The village was completely surrounded by vineyards.

Montreux on lake—wow! Snow in crevices.

We met a black woman singer who worked as a model but didn't like it. An older Swiss gentleman came on strong and bugged her, asking her if she wanted to see his flat in Lausanne. A young American photographer who "mostly does beauty" shots also talked to her. I was self-important: I love, I think, I feel. Touch, touch. Many friends in many ports. Mundane philosophy.

"It's always nice when you take a train and meet somebody you like, 'cause you don't always."

"Yes, it's nice to meet someone who can speak..."

Scotland

In Scotland, names for the Aviemore Clan Tartan Center: Scott, Roe, Sherwood, Robinson, Smith, Elliott, Flaherty, Strowbridge, Carmichael, Nelson, Gourley, Whitaker. [Ed. Note: Family lore tells that Sir Walter Scott is Carolyn's sixth great uncle. She and Jami were excited to visit his home in Scotland, Abbotsford House.]

Birds: fully musical sounds in all of England and Scotland. Rooks or ravens?

I rode in the back of the train with a good-looking gent (Leslie Howard type with strong features). He was well-dressed and on his way home from a business trip, checking stock in various West Coast cities. He caught a river trout a few days ago and was looking forward to it for dinner, though that wouldn't be until 9 p.m. We talked of accents and he said Inverness folk spoke perfect English without an "English" accent. We later learned Dubliners do, too. Boys from a football game got on and we loved how we couldn't understand a word they said. Should we have tried to speak their language, as we did in Spain?

Jami and I arrived at the bus station at 9:10 p.m. and an inspector told us where we could find a private hotel. We walked a block and a half by whole rows of old, clean houses. We went into the Windsor Hotel and got a back room overlooking horses, stone houses, and the sea. We went out for beer and brought back two cans of bitters, had our cob [bread] and cheese sandwiches in the room, and read.

We thought we'd miss the 10:00 a.m. bus, but even though we started breakfast at 9:15, we were at the bus station by 9:50. We arrived in Glasgow at 11:45 with the next bus set for 4:15 p.m. The station was surrounded by rubble in a crummy part of town; no greenery. I ran out of hair spray and looked a sight; Jami's teeth ached. Here the sky was a brilliant blue and sunny, but there were no picnics and nothing scheduled on Sunday, not even a movie. We walked up a dead street that was being made into a mall, but no shops—or liquor stores—were open yet.

We finally found a bar and shared a pint and fish and chips and ate in the middle of the street before heading back to the bus station for coffee. This was our first negative experience: Jami in pain, me unhappy. What a shame. But there was no sign of "Scotland" other than posters and the burr. The bus had big band 40s music like "I'm Beginning to See the Light" and other pleasant songs. Strange drinks were made, and we wanted to learn what they were. We used our bus pass to Inverness for the last time. We should have seen more of Ayr.

Glasgow was full of old ornate buildings covered with black and fronted by plastic shops or warehouses with garages below. We passed a book-maker and a large old building housing both the museum and an art gallery near the cathedral. Lots of litter and posters on the ground—trying to improve. Down the river, Clyde and Firth were lined with huge two- and three-story homes, and colorful sail boats docked on both sides. We stopped into the Green Kettle Tea Room for tea and scones as the grey sky lowered ahead.

On the drive back, we took a long, five-minute break at Loch Lomond. We tried to follow the map, but no towns were listed. It was a fun, roundabout trip. The lake ends by green pastures of sheep, sheer moors, rushing creeks, woods, waterfalls, and rocky land. It must be heavenly in the summer and a fisherman's paradise. The snow on the peaks was the best yet on our way to Oban. The trees were bare, and the people were handsome, a winter landscape.

The beautiful entrance to Oban was on the water, a lovely little fishing harbor. Sheep grazed the water's edge and the bus stopped in front of Caledonian Hotel. We walked in bedraggled. The girl at the desk said, "All booked up," but a handsome older gent with a pint informed us that the guest house around back had room. We walked to an ornate stone building. It had only one double bed left for $6.50 (including breakfast). It was a big room with a window over the bay. On the way, we saw an ad for Highland Piper and dancing that night, which wouldn't have known if we'd stayed in the Caledonian!

There were three baths in a row near our room in the hallway. We tried to do something with our hair and at 9:30 p.m. went to McIntosh's Kitchen to listen to black folk singers for half an hour. Then, a big retired chief piper of The Glasgow Pipe Band and a bemedaled 12-year-old lassie marched in and played on their bandstand. An accordion player followed, but at least played cultural music. The hotel was crowded, but we went back for lovely bed and awoke to rain and fog.

We drove north along what must be waterways. I felt so good, so at home, and took pictures of a castle on Loch Ness. We caught the train from Inverness to Aviemore and Pitlochry before our passes expired at midnight. Inverness is a small village, but a theme-park-like energy is emerging with ski lessons, riding, skating, climbing, Santa Claus barrel racing, and bumper cars. The center, too, has mostly tartans in ties, but with few kilts, cloth, or mufflers. We got on the computer to input our data on Scott, Robinson, Elliott, and Carmichael. Before boarding the train, we stopped in a bar for a pint for me and a gin for Jami's teeth.

On the train to Pitlochry, we ate beef burgers (buns better than ours) and drank rosé. We also bought extra bottles hoping to have a perfect day in Pitlochry. My heart was in the highlands. Snow was on the hills, but the air was fresh and balmy. The rocky hills were barren, but the heather is probably in bloom in the summer. The oceanside idyllic scenes of streams, pastures, and trees had a few farm houses. When we arrived in Pitlochry at 7:00 that evening, we were beside a beautiful gated garden and "Fisher's Hotel." We went in through the back door and took a room, tearing up to number 33 to get our boots on.

We noted a play at 8:00 p.m. and after walking the wrong way and then asking for help, we made it, sitting in the second row. It turned out to be "Private Lives" by Noel Coward. Darling theater full of all kinds of people.

We managed to get to a chemist's for life-saving hairspray (though still too weak) and medicine for Jami's teeth (ditto) before catching a train back on Saturday. A scruffy chef sat next to Jami and gulped from a pint of Scotch, apologizing that he'd been to a pub this late and his "head is a bit fuzzy." It was chilly out; the sun was up but the sky threatened clouds.

We had high hopes for sun in Edinburgh, but had to change at Perth because of a damaged tunnel. We sat across from a gorgeous sandy-haired, big-eyed youth who noted the young stag we saw leap over a pasture fence. He blushed when I said, "I hope they don't shoot them here." "I hope not, too," he said. He'd been to Florida for a month.

We took a stuffy carriage to Edinburgh, but found the largest, most efficient Info Center. Unfortunately, they booked us into an attic of a private hotel at the bottom of a steep hill with circular stairs. We strolled down to Grassmarket for gifts and up the steps to Royal Mile, but read that Holyrood House was closed. We discovered a great restaurant for dinner. A lonely single man sat opposite, but...

Walking home, we decided that one's impressions of a city depend a lot on one's accommodations. A feeling of expansion and beauty? Cramped and dull? Be careful of judgments. I was thinking of how I felt bummed at the beginning and could then look out over cluttered buildings and our garret with its sloping side windows. I looked at the rows of wild clouds, street lights and felt like I was in a scene from Dickens. I'm living in Edinburgh. My garret is like dozens of others. I'm a part of it, not a tourist.

An old woman alone, unafraid, and the constable shy. The yellow gaslights, the sloping roofs, the nightlife below. The castle at the end of the row, an old kirk near the block's end. Thank God for allowing me to see this!

Appendix B
Sample Scrapbook Pages

Tinyurl.com/cassadytips
for all full-sized images

Password: TopWithens

Carolyn Cassady's
1979 European Holiday

European Trains

Portugal......3–13
Spain..........14–45
Morocco.....46–51
Spain..........52–58
Portugal....59–74
Spain..........75–76
France........77–82

Spain................83–95
Italy..................96–103
Switzerland.....104
France............105–111
England...........112–132
Scotland.........133–145
England...........146–162

Britain

Portugal / Spain

Portugal

BY MOTORCOACH   22 DAYS

← your stomach -
what a lunch!

In a "typico" bistro
near Notre Dame we
ate Boef Baurguignonne(?)
bald boiled mushrooms,
whole, French fried
potatoes, ice cream
(French vanilla) & coffee.
Never suspecting the
eating ordeal that
awaited us for
dinner ......

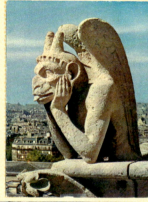

Notre Dame
Notre-Dame de Paris, on the spot where Celtic fishermen made their first camping ground, and Geneviève, the patron saint of the city, stood off the barbarian hordes of Attila with prayer and sword. Begun in 1163, completed in 1345, badly damaged during the revolution, restored by Viollet-le-Duc in the 19th century, Notre-Dame is one of the most beautifully proportioned of cathedrals, large enough to accommodate 9,000 people. Climb to the tower for a fuller appreciation of the architectural detail of the cathedral, as well as for a view of the heart of Paris.

NOTRE-DAME CATHEDRAL*

207

LONDON

LONDON THEATRE

St. Martin-in-the-Fields, overlooking Trafalgar Square, is the Royal Parish Church, dear to the hearts of many an Englishman, and especially the homeless who have found shelter in its crypt during many a cold winter night. The present classically inspired church, with its famous steeple, dates back to 1721. James Gibbs, a pupil of Wren's, is listed as its architect. The origins of the church go back to the 11th century. Among the congregation in years past was George I, who was actually a churchwarden, unique for an English sovereign. From St. Martin's vantage position on the theater district, it has drawn many actors to its door—none more notable that Nell Gwynne, the mistress of Charles II. On her death in 1687, she was buried here. Throughout the war, many Londoners rode out an uneasy night in the crypt, while blitz bombs rained down overhead. One, in 1940, blasted out all the windows.

Plays

*We walked past Whitehall &
#10 Downing St. dark, also. We
feel privileged to be there when
Maggie Thatcher was elected & we
saw her move in (accidentally) All
the British were loved her. Not the
Scots however. The* ★*IRA also.*

KIDS GALA 1979

Kids, a small and not very well known charity, has drawn together for the third time an International cast to take part in its Opera and Ballet Gala at the London Coliseum on May 6 at 19.30, in the presence of H.R.H. Prince Michael of Kent.

Victoria de Los Angeles will be taking part in the Gala for the second time. Teresa Berganza will be singing some Spanish Folk Songs and taking part in the Gala also for the second time will be the Bolshoi's Valentina Levko, Thomas Allen, Elizabeth Harwood, Raimund Herincx and Pauline Tinsley will be representing Great Britain. The Royal Ballet Company will be represented by Lesley Collier, Wayne Eagling, Stephen Jefferies and the Sadler's Wells Royal Ballet will dance a divertissement from *Coppélia*, and Peter Schaufuss will dance the celebrated *pas de deux* from *Le Corsaire*, one of the most spectacular in the ballet repertoire. London will also be seeing for the first time two of the leading young Bolshoi dancers, Nina Prokofieva and Andrei Kondratyev, and from Berlin to dance in London for the first time will be Igor Kosak and Heidrun Schwaarz.

The Gala will be introduced by amongst others Janet Suzman and Anton Dolin. The orchestra is The English National Opera and the conductors will be Sir Charles Groves and Anthony Twiner.

Kids is a national society for deprived and handicapped children. The charity has a centre in Northamptonshire which provides short term care and holidays for the mentally handicapped.

The KIDS Gala
at the London Coliseum
in the presence of H.R.H. Prince Michael of Kent
Please be seated
for 7.30 p.m.

The KIDS Gala
at the London Coliseum
in the presence of H.R.H. Prince Michael of Kent
Please be seated
by 7.25 p.m.

EVE. 7-30
MAY 6
SUNDAY

D 6

Dress Circle
£10.00 incl. VAT

Conditions see over   Aisle 1

A Gala of Opera and Ballet
In the presence of H.R.H. Prince Michael of Kent
Sunday, May 6th, 7.30 p.m. at the London Coliseum in aid of KIDS
Artists will include
VICTORIA DE LOS ANGELES
TERESA BERGANZA
ELIZABETH HARWOOD
RAIMUND HERINCX
VALENTINA LEVKO
PAULINE TINSLEY
ALAIN DUBREUIL
LESLEY COLLIER
WAYNE EAGLING
STEPHEN JEFFERIES
ANDREI KONDRATYEV
IGOR KOSAK
NINA PROKOFIEVA
PETER SCHAUFUSS
HEIDRUN SCHWAARZ
MARION TAIT
Members of the SADLER'S WELLS ROYAL BALLET and the children from ANNIE
*Members of the Bolshoi
Tickets £15.00, £10.00, £7.50, £6.50, £4.50, £3.50, £2.00
From: The Box Office, London Coliseum - Tel. 01-836 3161

HAYMARKET
Haymarket, SW1

Mon.-Fri.
Eves. 8.0
Sat. 4.30 & 8.0
Mon., Wed. 2.30

KEITH MICHELL, SUSAN HAMPSHIRE
in the new Sherlock Holmes Mystery
THE CRUCIFER OF BLOOD
by Paul Giovanni

THE CRUCIFER OF BLOOD. Keith Michell is Sherlock Holmes and Susan Hampshire the wretched lady in a saga involving stolen Indian treasure. A distinguished cast includes Edward Petherbridge and John Quentin and the only comedy this side of the whodunit; it does not change as the play progresses. Expect the River Thames, nothing more. This is a deft, highly satisfying spectacular. Evgs. at 20.00; Wed. at 14.30; Sat. at 16.30.

HAYMARKET THEATRE
Haymarket, SW1 (930 9832)

*We ordered champagne
at intermission to try + lure
up to the fancy-dressers.
They open a bottle & save
it for you on ice....
After the show we stood
outside waiting another look
at Prince Michael—but no.
No cabs—walked home.
at 11:30 AM. He passed in limo!*

Page 120 of 161

ANDALUSIA

Last Moorish stronghold: the mountainous Alpujarras region of Andalusia. Members of the *Guardia Civil*, or rural police, patrol a road on the south slopes of the snow-topped Sierra Nevada, 30 miles from the warm Mediterranean. After the fall of Granada in 1492, the Moors found refuge among these towering peaks.

Appendix C
Sample Original Diary Pages

ENGLAND

IN LONDON:

Buy "Pay-as-you-go" bus-pass & take 2 hr. tour. "Open-to-View" ticket

---

Leaving Paris — no one (Bank or change place) would cash my £ traveler's checks signed 3 — Boarded train to Boulogne & across from us is typico British bloke

checked coordinated tweeds & reading "Memoires of a Fox-Hunting Man" Welcome to England! Mr. Haggis on phone last eve said "Welcome Home" —

Language problem: So used to thinking "Now, how do I say that?" when on The. train, turni

Look up: Falcon Manor
u Skipton
decided to stay   26,400
another night —   10 000
were "knocked up" for   9 400
breakfast @ 9 —   18.600
2 had eggs,   123 000
fried bread, bacon   _____
                        187.400
= $230 — train from Fez to Paris
sausage, tomato & Iams here
pork/beans on toast with an egg!
Toast & Dundee of course &
coffee — We returned to Inf Center
for future cruises, bought book
on Brontïs & Kathleen wrapped
it for us, telling us of her
family in Haworth Re while —
"The Brontïs weren't the only
family w/ tragedy" was
her comment when I asked
if she ever interested in the
"My great grandfather u
the town teacher & cut their
hair" did give her pride —

Other Titles
from The Open Book Press

These poems take the reader from the Bay Area to Kansas to war-torn Korea, while also moving through a hallucinogenic realm of dreams and imagination.

"What a cosmic gift, a veritable cosmos of Berson's advanced pyrotechnic verse. Fasten your star-studded seatbelts! You're in for a grand ride!" —David Meltzer

Raw, visceral, and poetically charged, *Tiny Coffins* treats each page as just that, a tiny coffin of memory, facts of life, and the trials of family devotion.

"Exposes a universe of intimacies binding a daughter to her ailing mother, a series of dramatic snapshots recounting pained memories and illustrating how illness skews the everyday. Artful and engaging, with a powerful arc." —Jon Roemer

For almost five decades Yakshi has found joy and fulfillment contributing to her community's wellbeing and family's livelihood as a librarian and teacher. But it is poetry that has fueled the work and kept her alive.

"*Feminine Face of God* pulses with the intimacy and love that vibrates through all our relations, revealing our communion with the entire reality. These poems throb with life." —Diane Pendola